7 Lessons on Marriage
from the
Garden of Eden

JIM STERN

Copyright © 2016 by Jim Stern

All rights reserved.

No part of this book may be reproduced in any form or by any electronic or mechanical means, including information storage and retrieval systems, without written permission from the author, except for the use of brief quotations in a book review.

Edited and Formatted by Blake Atwood with
BA Writing Solutions: BlakeAtwood.com.

ISBN-13: 978-1540588166
ISBN-10: 1540588165

http://www.trexo.org

To Brooke,

The biggest lesson I have learned in our marriage to date is the wonder and joy of seeing life through someone else's eyes. You have helped me to appreciate many realities of life I never would have seen were it not for you. You continue to be a powerful demonstration to me that our Father's will for my life is "good, pleasing, and perfect."

I hope others are able to glean from this book that God's way for marriage works beautifully!

CONTENTS

INTRODUCTION: Life and Marriage on the Rock 1

1: SUBMIT: Follow the Same Leader 13

2: EMBRACE: Live as God Made You 31

3: DIAGNOSE: Know Your Sin 49

4: RELAX: Apply the Secret Ingredient 71

5: FIGHT: Engage in Spiritual Warfare 91

6: MERGE: Choose Oneness 107

7: JOURNEY: Learn to Road Trip Together 129

A Final Word 149

About the Author 153

ACKNOWLEDGMENTS

I live a crazy, on-the-branch-with-Jesus kind of life. I am dependent on Him for everything. So my life is full of ongoing stories of God's faithfulness. Sometimes He blesses me directly; many times His blessings come through others. I am grateful to those who have been sources of God's faithfulness to me to make this project work.

To Matt and Jessica Trozzo, John and Lindsey Lyons, and Dottie Collins, thank you for pre-reading this book and offering your wisdom and perspective. To those of you who have given financially, thank you. And to those of you who cover me and fill me with your prayers, thank you.

Living in the faithfulness of God is a wonderful, frightening, beautiful way to live. And I would not do it any other way.

With love,
Jim

INTRODUCTION
LIFE AND MARRIAGE ON THE ROCK

It is a heck of a thing for a man and woman to become a husband and a wife. New titles. New responsibilities. New complexities. New uncertainties. New emotions. New experiences. Massive change. No hiding. Complete vulnerability. Great possibility for blessing and joy. Learning how to build a relationship at the speed of life in the midst of war. Balance. Trust. Grace. Mercy. Patience . . . more patience. Father, Son, and Holy Spirit converging in the ongoing miracle of a man and woman becoming, and being, one.

Marriage is such an interesting phenomenon. How can something have so much potential for life and beauty and, at the same time, cause so much pain and suffering? Songs, poems, stories, movies, and paintings have all been created celebrating love in marriage. Yet, too often marriage can look like fighters inside the octagon at a mixed martial arts event.

If you're married, or have been married, you will know what I'm talking about when I say that when your marriage is strong, nothing else matters. Your career can be falling apart, but if your marriage is good, then you know things will be okay. But, when your marriage is bad or unstable, then nothing else matters. Work can be fantastic, but you will be miserable. That is the power of marriage.

Marriage is so powerful and so foundational that whole societies and civilizations will rise and fall based on the strength of the home.

In my opinion, one of the lowest points any person experienced in Scripture happened in the marriage between Job and his wife. In Job 1:1–2:8, we find out that Job was a righteous man who was tempted by Satan. Satan wanted to show God that Job was only righteous because God protected him and had given him a great life. Satan's premise was that loving God is easy when things are going well. God gave Satan permission to afflict Job.

Job lost everything: his wealth, his children, and his health. But, he never lost his faith. I believe his darkest moment came in Job 2:9 when his wife came to him and said, "Do you still hold fast your integrity? Curse God and die!" His wife took her support away from him.

Job was alone.

This is the power of marriage.

Marriage Has Become a Battlefield

Getting married puts you in a very vulnerable position. In giving yourself to another person, you are saying, "I'm giving you the power to build me up and to tear me down. I'm putting my life in your hands." Unfortunately, the evidence overwhelmingly cries out that we are doing far more tearing down than we are building up.

Marriage can be like a battlefield with land mines everywhere. For at least six hundred years, land mines have been a choice weapon in warfare. They are effective because they are buried in the ground. The opposition has no idea where they are. People who step on the mine have no idea they're about to be blown up. By 2007, improvised explosive devices (IEDs), a crude type of land mine, were responsible for 63 percent of coalition deaths in the Iraq war. That is a lot of destruction.

Spouses live in a field of land mines. When enough pressure is applied by a spouse—BOOM! Usually, the explosion will set off a chain reaction. One spouse's explosion sets off the other's and war has begun.

I do not use the Iraq war analogy lightly. The marriage battlefield is filled with real casualties, real pain, and real suffering. Statistics on divorce and the way those statistics are collected are debated. I have read some surveys that say 50 percent of first-time marriages end in divorce, some that say 40 percent, and some that say it is impossible to know exactly how many marriages divorce.

Unfortunately, we don't really need statistics to get a clear picture of the difficulty of marriage. All you have to do is consider how many people you know who are divorced. Each one of those divorces came about through a painful process of relational deterioration filled with fights and raw emotion: husbands and wives suffering long, lonely nights for months on end in anguish. Many of these divorces involve children.

Divorce is ugly and brutal. No one wins.

Regarding the research, let's be conservative and say that 40 percent of first marriages end in divorce. That means six out of ten first marriages will stay together. But the goal and design of marriage is not to be miserable and married. So let's subtract those still married but miserable. Of the six first marriages still together, how many would you say are miserable?

This is purely anecdotal, but you know a decent number of people. Based on how your married friends talk about their marriages, how many of them are miserable? The usual response I get is two to four. Of the six remaining married couples in our hypothetical illustration, two to four of those couples are miserable. So let's go in the middle and say that three couples are married but miserable. If we add the miserable to the divorced, we can surmise that 70 percent of first marriages will fail.

That means before a couple says, "I do," they only have a 30 percent chance of having a great marriage. That might be a good average in baseball, but in marriage that is brutal. And there is *no* correlation between how cute the couple is, or how much money they spend on their wedding, and how successful their marriage will be.

I use this "out-of-ten" exercise in my first pre-marital sessions with engaged couples. I do not do it to be harsh or to pour cold water on their love. I want them to grasp firmly the challenge of marriage. I'm sure some of those first-timers had some type of prenuptial agreement in case of divorce; however, the vast majority of people who say, "I do" do not do so planning on getting divorced. They think they're going to make it. They think the marriage statistics don't apply to them.

After all, they're *really* in love.

To add fuel to an already raging fire, the condition of marriage inside the church for those who say they believe in Jesus *is no better*.

What is going on?
Is there any hope?
Does marriage have to be a battlefield?
If so, why get married at all?

All about the Rock

Once, when I was watching a soccer game on TV, one of the commentators said, "Soccer is a really simple game, but the players can make it so complicated." The same can be said about marriage. Marriage is a simple reality, but husbands and wives make it so complicated.

Would God give us marriage so that we would have to live in a gender torture chamber? Did He design marriage for His own entertainment so He could watch men and women contort in painful ways? No and no.

God knew what He was doing when He created marriage. He has given us a surefire, undefeatable "formula" for a successful marriage. The formula works in all cases, for all time, in all places. The formula never promises a pain-free, difficulty-free, challenge-free marriage. That does not exist.

What the formula does guarantee is that if the husband and wife give themselves to it, their marriage will endure. They will not simply survive. Thirty, forty, and fifty years into marriage they will be happily married.

The formula is simple: when both the husband and wife surrender their lives to Jesus and follow Him, *according to Him, in all things*, then He will secure their lives together.

"According to Him, in all things" is the kicker in this formula. Too many people try to negotiate in their relationship with the Lord, somehow believing God has agreed to their terms. The conversation will go something like this: "God, here is the life I want to live and the plans I have. Bless them, please. In Jesus's name (because we have to add this to make it official), amen." Then they get angry when life doesn't work out according to their deal.

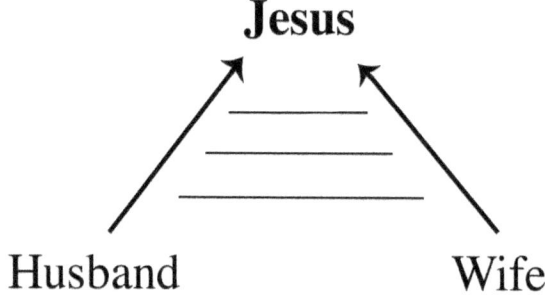

Figure 1: As the husband and wife seek Jesus, they grow closer to each other.

The formula is found in Jesus's teaching. His words on what it means to follow Him are straightforward:

> Therefore everyone who hears these words of Mine and acts on them, may be compared to a wise man who built his house on the rock. And the rain fell, and the floods came, and the winds blew and slammed against that house; and *yet* it did not fall, for it had been founded on the rock. Everyone who hears these words of Mine and does not act on them, will be like a foolish man who built his house on the sand. The rain fell, and the floods came, and the winds blew and slammed against that house; and it fell—and great was its fall. (Matthew 7:24–27, emphasis added)

Jesus promises that a person who follows Him, according to Him, in all things, will live a life that endures every storm. Both people, those on the Rock and those on the sand, are hit by storms. The formula does not prevent storms, but it does prevent catastrophic storm damage. But those who build their lives on the Rock endure. No storm can defeat them.

So, then, what happens when a man and woman who both live their lives on the Rock get married? Man on the Rock becomes husband on the Rock. Woman on the Rock becomes wife on the Rock. Single on the Rock becomes married on the Rock. Therefore, their marriage, even though continually hit by the harshness of life, endures!

Guaranteed.
Promised by Jesus Himself.
Only defeatable if He is defeatable.
Which isn't happening!

Notice that the rock is the *foundation* of the house. I believe this is the reason so many marriages do not make it, even when they "believe" in Jesus. While they may have Jesus in their lives, He is not the foundation. He may be a room, a floor, or a decorative cross on a wall, but He is not the foundation. Or, in other cases, He may be only part of the foundation. When He is only part of the foundation, a husband or a wife do not believe in everything God's Word teaches about the foundation of life and marriage.

The marriage Rock formula works when both husband and wife live faithfully in relationship with the Father, Son, and Holy Spirit. Man follows the Lord in all things, humbling himself, allowing the Spirit to conform him into the image of Jesus, walking in the will of the Father regardless of where He leads. The woman seeks the face of Christ as a daughter of God, filled with the Spirit, following the will of her Father. The two marry and learn how to walk faithfully together.

The goal of this book is to lay a marital foundation which is faithful to Jesus that will endure as Jesus promises it will.

What is Your Foundation?

If we are going to deal with foundations, we must go to *the* foundation. Genesis 1:1–3:24 records the foundations of life and marriage. These verses have abundant meat that is often overlooked. In these three chapters we first find God, the order of creation, time, light, heaven, angels, planets and solar systems, animals, plants, man, and marriage.

We also find the real presence of evil.

We will discover that the opening chapters of the Bible give us seven foundational insights into life and marriage. Understanding and embracing these insights will lay the foundation Jesus intended when He spoke the words recorded in Matthew 7. Some of these you will already know, some you will be aware of, and others will be new. Whether you are engaged, considering getting engaged, have been married a while, or have been married a long time, I believe you will find many powerful insights that will help you experience everything God intends you to have. And it will help you help others as God brings them into your life.

I remember being very confused by the sequence of these verses. They did not seem to fit together. Later, I learned that Genesis 1:1–2:3 is a big picture presentation of creation. Genesis 2:4–3:24 picks up the story from the creation of man, adding detail we are not given in the big picture. So Genesis 1:1–2:3 covers the seven days of creation. Genesis 2:4–2:24 starts on day six and keeps going. This will be helpful for you to understand the Scripture and this study as some of what we are going to cover will be "out-of-order."

Furthermore, the order that Adam and Eve experienced life is different than our order. They were born in innocence and fell into sin. We are born into sin and only experience innocence through Jesus. The material is presented in the order in which we experience it. So Chapters 2–6 of this book cover truths and issues we encounter before marriage that we bring into marriage. These truths and issues do not end when we get married, but in order to consider them we need to deal with them before, and in, marriage.

A Brief Word to Men

I offer a word to men because, generally speaking, men are much more susceptible to minimize the power and significance of marriage.

Don't buy the lie that marriage isn't worth investing in, spending time on, and fighting for. Too many of us have been sold a bill of goods that says our jobs are to be in the workplace making a name for ourselves.

Real men don't sit and talk with their wives.
Real men don't make their marriages a priority.
Real men leave the marriage stuff to their wives.

Garbage.

How about this?

Real men recognize the glory, power, and blessing of marriage. Real men, those who are *wise*, see the absolute glory of what God has done in marriage and get to work building a phenomenal relationship with their wives. Real men reject the machismo, too-cool attitude we're taught to believe.

Real men walk in absolute humility in the presence of the God of all creation, seeking His face, each man embracing his own identity as a son of God and pouring himself out, even unto death, to serve his King.

In this, men intentionally work on their marriages, asking God to make them into better husbands and blessings for their wives.

I love wedding receptions. They are usually filled with great hope and love as everyone celebrates the new couple. One of the common games played at the reception is Last Couple Standing. The DJ will call out, "Everyone who has been married less than ten years, please leave the dance floor." You know this game. Then he will go on to those married less than twenty, thirty, or forty years. Finally, the couple married the longest will still be dancing. Usually, the couple will have been married fifty-plus years! Sometimes the couple has been married sixty years! And they're still dancing!

That is God's desire for marriage: sixty years and still dancing! That is His goal for you. That is my goal for you. It is possible. Sixty years and sitting on a porch, or walking through a mall holding hands, still madly in love. Whether you can see it or not is irrelevant. Do you believe God can do it? He can. He has real hope and real solutions.

I pray this book will offer insight into God's creation of life and marriage in a way that will totally transform you and your marriage.

Dig into it.

Let the Spirit of God work within you.

CHAPTER 1
SUBMIT: FOLLOW THE SAME LEADER

One day when my son was in the second grade, he asked me to play four square with him. I used to love four square when I was a kid, so I joyfully accepted the challenge!

Things were going well until he picked up the ball and said, "Catches and holds." Then he spiked the ball and knocked me out! Not only was I out, but I was confused. I said, "What is catches and holds?" I had never heard of such things in four square. He went on to explain these rules. I thought they were silly and unnecessary.

Even though we were playing the same game, we were playing by different rules, and it wasn't working. For us to have a great time playing four square together, we had to agree on the rules!

Both spouses must follow the same leader.
The keyword for this lesson is **submit**.

For marriage to work, a husband and wife need to agree on who or what is their truth and authority. It should be easy to see what the result will be in a marriage where spouses believe differently, pursue differently, and live differently. In a healthy marriage, both spouses follow the same leader.

God as Creator and Designer

Thankfully, joyfully, wonderfully, God makes it very clear that He is the Creator of all things. Genesis 1:1 says, "In the beginning, God created the heavens and the earth." Genesis 1:26 says, "Then God said, 'Let Us make man in Our image, according to our likeness.'" God made everything, including man, woman, marriage, and family.

John 1:3 says, "All things came into being through Him, and apart from Him nothing came into being that has come into being." There is nothing in all of creation that was not created by God. From the farthest star and galaxy to the smallest molecule on Earth, from the reaches of Heaven to the last angel, God has made everything in creation both seen and unseen.

God made man. God made woman. God made marriage. Consequently, as Creator, God is truth and authority in all things. As truth, God is *the* definer of life and all things in life. As authority, God's will is *the* path of life. Whatever God says about life and marriage is true and authoritative according to the way He designed life and marriage to be.

Pontius Pilate famously asked Jesus, "What is truth?" (John 18:38). He voiced his own frustration from his experience with the elusiveness of truth. Conversely, earlier in Jesus's ministry, Jesus said, "If you continue in My word, then you are truly disciples of Mine; and you will know the truth, and the truth will make you free" (John 8:31–32).

The world lives in a shroud of lies and deceit. God is truth and the only source of truth. Whatever God says about whatever God says is true. God is the definer of life, gender, roles, marriage, parenting, success, happiness, blessing, morality, economics, science, arts, music, finances, healing, the universe, eternal life, and everything else.

God has given us the Bible as His revelation to man. In addition to Scripture being the source of divine revelation, Scripture is God's dictionary. In Scripture, our Creator God gives His creation definitions: His truth about life and marriage.

In addition to truth, God is also the authority. He made creation according to His plan, and creation works when His plan is followed. With respect to those who give their lives to Jesus, the Apostle Paul writes in Ephesians 1:11, "In Him, also we have obtained an inheritance, having been predestined according to His purpose *who works all things after the counsel of His will*" (emphasis added). As Creator, God is the authority. Life and marriage work according to His plan.

God as the source of truth and authority should be a great relief to those on the journey of marriage: "The God of All Creation has a plan for life and marriage that works fantastically. Let's follow Him!" Can you imagine what a marriage would look like between two people joyfully submitted to God and His plan for their lives?

If only we could let it be that simple! Unfortunately, like many things in life, we love to make things complicated. The reality is that many of us have major obstacles when it comes to living by someone else's truth and authority—even God's.

I asked an engaged couple if they believed marriage was designed by God. They eagerly said yes. Then I said that believing in God's design means submitting to God's authority and asked if either one of them had issues with authority. The woman immediately declared, "I am a control freak and have major authority issues!" At least she was willing to admit it.

So what are your issues? Why is it difficult for you to hear the words of God, believe them, and act on them? Why do you struggle trusting your Father? As we will see, having unresolved truth and authority issues in marriage is going to cause significant problems.

Two Obstacles to Submitting to God's Truth

We can be very opinionated people. All you have to do is read through the comments section of any article posted on the Internet to discover the depth and passion people have about their opinions. To embrace God's definitions for life and marriage requires a person to walk away from every other contrary definition or opinion they've ever had.

1. Entrenched, Incorrect Definitions
There are at least two obstacles people have to submitting to God's truth. The first obstacle is entrenched, incorrect definitions. Our beliefs have been shaped in our lives for years by a variety of influences. Surrendering those definitions and embracing others can be quite chal-

lenging. For example, a person may have been raised to define success as being as highly educated as possible. But God does not define success through education. In the Lord, success is defined by faithfulness. Beauty is defined as an internal condition of the heart. Sex is defined as an intimate act reserved for a married man and woman. God's definitions are not just one option of many from which to choose. If we accept God as creator, then God's definitions are according to the way God has *designed* life and marriage to be. Entrenched, incorrect definitions are significant obstacles to walking in God's truth.

2. Feelings

Second, feelings are another major obstacle to living out God's truth. Many people believe that if they feel something it must be true. To deny their feelings is to invalidate the person's experience. This sounds nice, but in the Lord it can be flat-out wrong. If we accept God as Creator, then we accept that truth exists. We become people led by truth, not by feelings. Our first question must be, "What is the truth in every given situation?" Then we feel according to truth. So just because a person does not "feel" successful does not mean they are not successful. Just because a person "feels" unloved does not mean they are unloved.

Our culture seems to be infested with the belief that all feelings are legitimate and must be validated. This is wrong and dangerous. Consider a husband and wife together in a room. He gets up and leaves without saying anything to her. She gets her feelings hurt because what he did was unloving toward her. She pulls away from him for the rest of the day until evening, when she expresses her anger at what he did and demands that he validate her feelings. However, what she could not see was that a close friend waved him out of the room with a look of panic on his face. The wife blew up because she had responded to an incomplete understanding of the situation.

If we embrace God as Creator, then we must be people of truth. We live according to truth and seek truth in the situations and issues we are confronted with. This does not mean we do not feel. Not at all! In the Lord, we feel fully and appropriately. As the God of truth, God is full of emotions, properly defines them, and shows us how to correctly experience them!

Three Obstacles to Submitting to God's Authority

Full-length books can be written on every reason people have authority issues. Dealing with all of them is beyond the scope of this book. We will consider three. If none of these resonate with your authority struggle, then ask the Holy Spirit to show you what is keeping you from trusting your Father.

1. Fear

Do you fear submitting to your Father because you fear His way is not going to be what you want? Breathe. It won't be! In fact, it won't even be close. But it will be far better. And it will be better in ways you could never foresee and better in places you may only be vaguely aware even exist in you.

Scripture teaches us that "God is love" (1 John 4:9). The Father, Son, and Holy Spirit exist in perfect love with each other. When you give your life to Jesus, you are not just connected with them, you are brought into Trinitarian love! The Father, Son, and Holy Spirit equally, perfectly love you. They desire you. They wait to meet with you, to bless you, and to lead you. Jesus's death and resurrection demonstrate the lengths they've gone to because of their love for you.

Jesus did not die on the cross to make your life boring.
And He did not die on the cross to make your life comfortable.
But He did die on the cross so that you could have life.

In following God's plan you will experience pain, suffering, great challenges, and difficulties. But in God's plan you will experience a richness of life and blessing you could never know any other way. There is no other way to life that remotely comes close to life in the Lord.

Look at the invitation God gives to Israel in Jeremiah 6:16: "Stand by the ways and see and ask for the ancient paths, where the good way is, and walk in it; And you will find rest for your souls." God tells Israel to compare all the different options available for how to live life. There are many different ways you can choose to live. God does not naively hide Israel from them and somehow "force" Israel to choose Him. He says, "Hey, there are many different ways. Evaluate them. Really evaluate them. Look at the people who are living according to those ways. Do they have rest? Is there peace in their souls? Don't be deceived by outward appearances. Let your standard be peace in the soul. Now, based on that, how do they look? There is a way—a good way, an ancient way— that when you walk in it you will experience rest in your soul." There is a better, brilliant way.

God's way of life is better than any other way.
God's way of marriage is better than any other way.
God's way of family is better than any other way.
God's way of _____ is better than any other way.

When was the last time you were disappointed because someone recommended a place to you that was no good? You tried a restaurant that was supposed to be great and it was terrible. You went to a mechanic who was supposed to be excellent and he did poorly. No one likes to be disappointed. **The brilliant reality of following God is that you will never be disappointed.** Ever. Romans 10:11 promises, "For the Scripture says, 'Whoever believes in Him will not be disappointed.'" When you obey God you will not be disappointed.

I was raised in the military. My dad served twenty-three years in the United States Air Force. Authority is not an issue in the military. They all understand it well. Military authority has nothing to do with love. You do what you do because you are told to do it.

Conversely, submitting to godly authority has everything to do with love. Jesus says in John 14:23, "If anyone loves Me, he will keep My word." For Jesus, obeying is what love does. Naturally and organically, love produces obedience. Galatians 4:4 says, "But when the fullness of the time came, God (the Father) sent for His Son."

You can imagine the conversation. At the right time in all of history, the Father "turns" toward the Son and says, "It is time for You to go my Son." The Son knows His Father loves Him and He loves His Father. Further, the Son knows the Father is the One with the plan. So the Son says, "Okay" and goes. Love obeys. To believe in God is to be in a love relationship with the Father, Son, and Holy Spirit where we obey the Father's will because He loves us and we love Him.

2. Selfishness

You want what you want! If you want to drive, you drive. If you want to eat, you eat. If you want to stop, you stop. If you want the air conditioning on low, then it is going on low and everyone else in the car will just have to deal with it. Life is about you, your comfort, and your vision.

Selfishness constantly wreaks havoc in marriage. A husband really wants to be successful in his career. He justifies his hours and time away from the family by believing, "I'm making more money to take care of my family." He knows it is all about him. When his wife says anything, he gets angry and accuses her of not understanding. His response shows that he believes she is in his life to help him accomplish his vision.

Or, a woman has a very clear picture of the house and family she wants. She constantly corrects her children and her husband and justifies her behavior by saying, "Manners and cleanliness are important." She knows it is all about her projecting the image she wants to have. She believes her husband and children are in her life to help her accomplish her vision

Selfishness is a major enemy of submission.

If these couples go to counseling, their selfishness may be addressed, but more than likely their issues in submitting to God's authority will not be touched. Yet, the issues they're facing with each other are merely symptomatic of deeper root issues with regard to each of them embracing God's authority over their lives and marriage.

As you see in the above examples, and may know from experience, selfishness produces control issues. You may be a control freak, or you may be married to one. (I've often wondered but have never really wanted to find out, what happens when two control freaks marry each other?)

I once overheard a woman describe how strict she is with her kids. Then she said, "I'm just a control freak" and laughed! Ugh. We do not like to surrender control. Oftentimes marriage can dissolve into a constant arm-wrestling match for control. Neither person wants to give in, or one spouse is so tired of the other's pressing they just give up. Control is a very bad ingredient for a successful marriage. The great reality about submitting to God is that neither the husband nor the wife are in control! Both ought to live by deferring to God and His leadership in all things.

When you wade out into the ocean, you begin in one place, but the current quickly takes you down the shoreline. Before you know it, you cannot see where you were. The current of selfishness is so strong that you need to anchor your submissiveness or you're going to drift away.

The strongest anchor is Jesus. He lived in continual submission to His Father. "I glorified You on the earth, having accomplished the work which You have given Me to do" (John 17:4). Jesus did not live for Himself. He followed His Father's will. Without question, He lived the richest, most satisfying, powerful, and restful life in history. Submission was part of His secret! There are many times while seeking to follow God's leading that you are going to need to look to Jesus and say, "I really am struggling to follow You in this Father. But, if Jesus did it, then I accept this is the way of life."

Looking to Jesus should also work toward correcting your overall belief about control and selfishness. Those attitudes are wrong and unhealthy for life or marriage. His life sheds light on the beauty of humility, grace, and selflessness, exposing control and selfishness for the lies they are.

So, the man driven by success to build his reputation, who excuses working extra hours under the lie that "I will make more money for the family," is freed by Jesus to live selflessly by putting his career in the hands of the Lord. Likewise, the woman who manipulates her family so she can have a picture-perfect home and family life is freed by Jesus to live in the peace of God's building work.

Allowing Jesus to be your anchor will help secure you in a posture of submission to the Lord.

3. The Past
This is perhaps the most difficult hurdle to leap when learning how to submit to God's authority. Some of us have had horrible past experiences with authority that have created a profound distrust in us. We have major issues with our moms, dads, grandparents, teachers, bosses, or others. This can be particularly damaging when the people involved are church leaders or those claiming some kind of Christian maturity. That's a brutal and unfortunate reality of life, and our resultant emotions can be overwhelming.

If this is you, know that our Father is gracious and has an amazing ability to pick up your hands in His and walk you through the most traumatic of experiences to places of healing and restoration you cannot see on your own. It is always wise to prayerfully seek out skilled counseling to help you. You are not alone. God has not left you and He has not forgotten you. He has people who will listen, care, and understand.

In the biblical story of the young teenager Joseph, his ten older brothers sold him into slavery. They abandoned Joseph and lied to their dad by telling him Joseph was dead. In time, Joseph ended up in Egypt where he was wrongly accused of rape and imprisoned twice. If there's any person in Scripture who has a reason not to trust authority, it's Joseph. However, he never let his circumstances define God. In spite of everything that happened to him, he knew God loved him and was faithful.

Eventually Joseph was selected by Pharaoh to be the Number Two man in all of Egypt. His brothers appealed to the Egyptian government for some food because of a famine in their land. This brought them face-to-face with the man they had abandoned. Joseph could have been full of anger and easily order their execution. He did not. God had taken great care of him. In Genesis 50:20, Joseph said to his brothers, "As for you, you meant evil against me, but God meant it for good in order to bring about this present result, to preserve many people alive." Joseph did not allow what those in authority did to him to define him, and he did not allow it to define God.

You do not have to let what those in authority did to you define you or define God. He loves you and is faithful to you. If you need counseling from someone gifted to help you walk through what you have been through, prayerfully seek it out.

If you're married to someone in this condition, be extremely gentle. Lean daily and heavily on the Holy Spirit to give you the grace and compassion you're going to need. Do not rush. Let the Spirit gently remove your vision of your life and replace it with God's vision so that you can faithfully minister to your spouse. Pray for God to send someone into your life who has experience in this and cultivate a healthy, Christ-centered relationship with them. There is a way through where you are, but it's not your way. And, it will require things of you that only the Holy Spirit can give you.

The book of Habakkuk is about the prophet Habakkuk struggling with God's plan. In Habakkuk 1:1–4, he's frustrated because he cannot see God working at all. Habakkuk 1:5–11 records God telling Habakkuk what His plan is. Habakkuk replies in 1:12–17 by telling God he does not like God's plan! The great thing about this prophet is that he takes his struggles to God.

It is okay to struggle with God's plan—just struggle *with* God about His plan. Be careful that your authority issues do not turn you away from God. Bring them to Him and let Him speak. Be honest. Unload. He will meet you where you are and perfectly walk with you to His place of grace.

With an agreed-upon authority, a husband and wife can seek truth and direction together. While there will still be plenty of opportunities for differences of opinion, arguments, and uncertainties, looking to the Lord gives the couple the benefit of a framework, principles, and resources to find answers.

Allowing God to identify and deal appropriately with the truth and authority issues you have is a great start to personal and relational healthiness. In some issues a person will need compassion and ministry. In others, a person will need to be woken up to the arrogance of their ways. If you're serious about succeeding in your marriage, then soberly ask God to help you.

Relying on the Sources of His Authority

We live in an information world. Through the Internet you can read article after article on any subject you can dream of. New studies are constantly coming out purporting to give wisdom for life in every area imaginable. You can spend hours and days and months consuming the latest this or that. For those who believe in the Father, Son, and Holy Spirit, we are blessed to look to Scripture as our information source. Consider the richness of the promised blessing for one who cultivates intimacy with God, in part, by spending regular time in His Word:

- Joshua 1:8 says, "This book of the law shall not depart from your mouth, but you shall meditate on it day and night, so that you may be careful to do according to all that is written in it; for then you will make your way prosperous, and then you will have success."

- Psalm 1:1–3 says, "How blessed is the man who does not walk in the counsel of the wicked, nor stand in the path of sinners, nor sit in the seat of scoffers! But his delight is in the law of the Lord, and in His law he meditates day and night. He will be like a tree firmly planted by streams of water, Which yields its fruit in its season And its leaf does not wither; And in whatever he does, he prospers."

- Psalm 19:7 says, "The law of the Lord is perfect, restoring the soul; The testimony of the Lord is sure, making wise the simple."

- 2 Timothy 3:16 says, "All Scripture is inspired by God and profitable for teaching, for reproof, for correction, for training in righteousness; so that the man of God may be adequate, equipped for every good work."

For the one who believes, Scripture is full of life and is joyfully followed.

When a man and woman are surrendered to God and His Word for their lives, they will regularly seek counsel through His Word. If you get lost on a road trip you look to your GPS for direction. In marriage, do not wait until you get lost to read His Word. "Let the word of Christ richly dwell with you" (Colossians 3:16). "Your word is a lamp to my feet and a light to my path" (Psalm 119:105).

Make Scripture *the* go-to source for direction and wisdom in all things. When disputes, decisions, and confusion happen, the couple will remember the Word and look to God in His Word for help. This is fantastic! You do not have to look to the latest study on parenting, gender issues, or marital roles. You look to God in His holy, eternal, perfect Word. You do not have to make decisions in fear. You can make them in the confidence that comes from knowing you and your spouse are making them according to God.

In addition to seeking God's wisdom in the Word, you will benefit by studying topical Bible studies. I also highly recommend that you seek and develop relationships with brothers and sisters in Christ who have been married a long time. You can avoid so many problems in your marriage by learning from others and leaning on them. Certainly, you need to be a part of a great church with a pastor who teaches Scripture.

Whatever you do, seek wisdom from God and His Word for your marriage. Heed the counsel of Solomon to his son in Proverbs 3:7–8: "Do not be wise in your own eyes; Fear the Lord and turn away from evil. It will be healing to your body and refreshment to your bones."

Before Marriage

A major part of the dating/courting process needs to be spent discovering where a person stands on their submission to God's leading. Simply "believing" in God or going to church does not rise to the level of what God says following Him means.

Does the person seek after the Lord and His will for their lives? Do they love the Lord and His ways for their life? Is that love seen in their love for themselves and others? How do they make decisions? How much does God impact their life? What kind of relationship do they have with the Father, Son, and Holy Spirit? What examples do they have of God leading them in their lives?

Do not compromise in this. You are going to pay for it if you do. It will be far better for you to be single than to be married to someone who does not share your passion for the Lord.

Conclusion

Being together on the authority issue is huge for a successful marriage. God's way of life is filled with rich abundance. When a husband and wife follow Him together they will experience blessings they never knew possible. Difficulties will still come. Life is hard. Nevertheless, when a husband and wife both "dwell in the shelter of the Most High" (Psalm 91:1), they will live His victory together.

Lean into Him. Share your authority issues with Him. Share your authority issues with your spouse, betrothed, or significant other. Just because you have authority issues does not mean you cannot be in a relationship. Be honest about them. Let the Lord heal you. Learn the beauty and joy of submission. Watch what He will do and feel how high He will lift you.

CHAPTER 2
EMBRACE: LIVE AS GOD MADE YOU

The most powerful earthquake ever recorded happened on May 22, 1960, in Valdivia, Chile. The quake measured a 9.5 on the moment magnitude scale. The next most powerful earthquake happened in 1964 in Alaska and measured 9.3. The Valdivian quake caused local tsunamis with waves up to eighty-two feet. New Zealand, Australia, Japan, the Philippines, and Hawaii all felt the effects. Hilo, Hawaii was hit with thirty-five-foot waves. The United States Geological Survey estimated the quake caused 5,700 deaths and $400–800 million in damage.[1]

The devastation we experience from an earthquake comes from something that happens below the surface. The earth's plates, which we cannot see, shift and begin wreaking havoc on what we can see. The internal instability of the earth produces damaging effects.

---

[1] Wikipedia, "1960 Valdivia earthquake," https://en.wikipedia.org/wiki/1960_Valdivia_earthquake

While you and I do not have plates shifting inside of us, we are internally unstable. And, like earthquakes, our internal instability causes severe damage to ourselves and others. Unlike earthquakes which strike and fade, man's internal instability can last for a lifetime and cause ongoing damage.

This *significantly* impacts marriage. In God's math, 1+1=1 at the altar. The man says, "This is who I am. I would like to join together with you." The woman says, "This is who I am. I would like to join together with you." And they are joined together to become one new creation that has never existed before.

But how well do the man and woman really know themselves? When Jane and Bill marry, how well does Jane really know Jane? How well does Bill really know Bill? How clear are they on the question of who they are as individuals? Invariably, fights happen in marriage because neither person knows themselves all that well. Instability has married instability. And, to add to the fun, neither one is fully aware of how unstable they are!

Marriage can force couples to discover who they are as man and woman. I say "can" because many will not care about discovering and will quit. This is unfortunate. Quitting is even more unfortunate when the answers to the "Who am I?" question are readily available. One of the benefits of walking with God is that He has already defined this for us. When a person converts from following the world to walk with Jesus, they shift from seeing themselves according to the world to seeing themselves as God sees them.

Embracing this new perspective, any man or woman has the ability to feel great about themselves because of who God is, what He says about them, and what He is doing in them!

Live as God made you.
The keyword for this lesson is **embrace**.

There is a difference between knowing truth and embracing truth. To embrace means "to take or receive gladly or eagerly; accept willingly."[2] By embracing, we move beyond an intellectual agreement *with* to a whole receiving *of*. Knowing does not transform; embracing does. What we embrace becomes who we are. God made every one of us according to His original design. You are built to work in the way that God built you to work. Embracing His design helps you become fully, truly you.

God lays out five foundational truths in Genesis 1–2 that begin to tell the story of who He has made you to be. Each of these truths is an essential pillar to your identity. Take any one away and you're going to suffer the consequences in instability.

1. You are made in the image of God.
"Let Us make man in Our image, according to Our likeness" (Genesis 1:26).

What is the main distinction between angels, animals, and humanity? Unlike angels and animals, men and women are made in the *image of God*. "Let Us make man in Our image, according to Our likeness . . . God created man in His own image, in the image of God He created them; male

---
[2] "embrace," http://www.dictionary.com/browse/embrace

and female He created them" (Genesis 1:26–27). Three times in two verses God makes sure it is known that He made man in His image. He said it forward: "God created man in His own image." He said it backwards: "In the image of God He created them." Whatever way you want to turn it, man was made and designed in the image of God.

You have been made in the image of God.
In the image of God, *you* have been made!

In the beginning before there was anything, there was the Father, Son, and Holy Spirit. They began the creative process. They made time, space, heaven, the universe, angels, light, earth, and everything on the earth. At the end of that process was their crowning achievement: you! Man stands alone in all of creation as the only entity made in the image of God. The universe is vast, comprised of hundreds of thousands of galaxies and countless numbers of stars and planets. Yet in all of the expanse, man exists as *the* image of the Creator.

It's staggering to consider all of the time, money, and emotion people spend trying to build their image when they can simply *embrace* their God-image. Diets, surgeries, exercise plans, extra work hours, drugs, sleeping around, buying too big of a house, gossip, overachieving, and so much more time and money wasted trying to feel good about one's self. This list can keep going and going.

Years turn into generations and generations into cultures. Whole industries are built on the premise that they can build an image for you that will satisfy your soul. Yet, none of it works! No one is satisfied. And, in the midst of all of this "image-quaking," a man and a woman are supposed to get married and live happily ever after!

Insanity.

Do you see this? The reason nothing else works is because *nothing else is good enough!* Nothing else rises to the magnitude and the majesty that you are made in the image of God. To what or to whom does that compare? You are made in the image of Mercedes-Benz? You are made in the image of the United States in the twenty-first century? You are made in the image of a bunch of marketing executives on Madison Avenue in New York City? What a bunch of garbage.

Why compromise? Why waste another moment of another day and another penny of another dollar on junk that will not work? Why not throw all of that away, every bit of it, and firmly grasp the truth that you are a created child of the Almighty God made in His holy and perfect image?

When you embrace God's image as the standard for your life, you are able to see what the truth is and what is a lie. Truth: you are made in the image of God. Lie: everyone else and everything else that says you are something less than the image of God. Now, to the extent that others have told you something else or made you feel something else, they're wrong! To the extent that you have told yourself something else or made yourself feel something else, you're wrong!

Go back to the previous lesson: Who is your authority? If God is your authority, then receive His words and reject the others. He is *the* image authority. Let His love and the truth of His words forcefully strike down every lie and event that has told you that you're something less than His image-bearer. You no longer have to be defined by anyone or anything else.

Instead of being image-needy, image-damaged, or image-confused, you can live image-strong.

2. You were made body and spirit.

"Then the Lord God formed man of dust from the ground, and breathed into his nostrils the breath of life; and man became a living being" (Genesis 2:7).

God's answer to the "Who am I?" question continues. In addition to being made in God's image, men and women are made in what John Cooper calls a "holistic duality."[3] Holistic duality is the understanding that you have been designed with a body *and* a spirit.[4] We see this in Genesis 2:7. There was dirt, then God formed man from the dirt. Man stood as lifeless dirt. (Some of us have not progressed much!) Then God breathed life into him and he came alive. The word "breath" in the Hebrew means spirit. It was not until God breathed spirit into man that he came alive. But, God's breath was breathed into a physical body.

Man and woman have been designed as both body and spirit. The interrelationship between your body and spirit is holistic. In other words, you cannot discern where one stops and the other starts. Consequently, your body affects your spirit and your spirit affects your body. This understanding is critical as it sheds light on why so much of what we do to feel great just doesn't work. Furthermore, knowing that we are both

---

[3] John W. Cooper, Body, Soul, and Life Everlasting: Biblical Anthropology and the Monism-Dualism Debate (Grand Rapids: Wm. B. Eerdmans Publishing, 1989).

[4] There is a debate about whether we are actually two parts: body/soul, or three parts: body/soul/spirit. This is not the place for that debate. My only intent here is to present the general teaching that we are more than a physical body. For additional reading, see Body, Soul, Life Everlasting by John Cooper or Wayne Grudem's Systematic Theology.

body and mind expands our understanding of potential causes for the issues in our lives.

People who work out vigorously and are in prime physical condition may still feel miserable. Other people who believe strongly in Jesus and know the Word of God, yet do not exercise, diet, or get good sleep, may also be miserable. Both are incomplete. Why? Because God has designed us as body and spirit.

A person who struggles with anxiety may be prescribed medication. While the medication helps, they never feel right. Unfortunately, they may have never considered that their anxiety may have a spiritual cause that can be easily remedied by learning correct prayer techniques or engaging in spiritual warfare. Another person may deny that there are any physical causes for depression. Their solution is to "pray and trust the Lord." But God has shown us that there can be physical causes of depression, and He has gifted men and women to create remedies.

Without a proper understanding of holistic duality, men and women are left to satisfy their instability in ways that are not designed to work. Oftentimes marriage becomes one of those solutions people believe will be the missing piece of their lives. There will be a lot of disappointment in those marriages when the man or woman discovers that their spouse cannot quiet their instability.

You are a holistic duality. Made in the image of God, you will find the deep satisfaction you desire as you rest in your relationship with the Father, Son, and Holy Spirit. God will minister to the whole person, leading you in the fullness of life in every area of your life. This is a powerful reality of God's design for both men and women. God intends you to reap wonderful benefits from holistic duality as you live in connection with Him.

Being made body and spirit is the second of five pillars essential to your identity.

3. *We were made male and female.*
"God created man in His own image, in the image of God He created him; male and female He created them" (Genesis 1:27).

In His perfect wisdom, God made humanity male and female. When Adam woke from his God-given nap he was amazed at who stood before him. Adam and Eve were to be together in deep intimacy, enjoying God's faithfulness *together* in the way God made marriage to work. They were to tend the garden of Eden, produce children, build a family, and worship the Lord harmoniously. God's design for man and woman was, and is, beautiful.

But, why the genders? Why not just make man or woman? In all the confusion, controversy, and pain gender issues have caused, why couldn't God have done something different?

The immediate answer is obvious: family. One of the unique features of male and female as image-bearers of God is their ability to build families. God made man male and female so they could experience the wonder of co-creating life with God. Then, man and woman could experience the wonder of nurturing the life they co-created. The family unit of husband, wife, and children mirrors the Trinitarian family of

Father, Son, and Holy Spirit. Angels do not reproduce. There is a finite number and no more are being made. Animals reproduce, but their reproduction is unlike man's in one important way.

In addition to genders being made for family building, God made humanity male and female for lifelong intimacy. Describing the lifelong condition of marriage, Jesus says in Matthew 19:6, "So they are no longer two, but one flesh. What therefore God has joined together, let no man separate." Neither angels nor animals enjoy such intimacy.

Divorce is not a part of God's gender design. God made male and female so that both could enjoy lifelong intimacy, vulnerability, and love with each other just as the Father, Son, and Holy Spirit enjoy intimacy with each other. Marital intimacy is a reflection of Trinitarian intimacy.

The experience of husband and wife in intimacy, procreation, and family building are divine, holy activities that only God and His image-bearers can do.

How far we have fallen. How confused and controversial the genders have become. What a mess. God's Word is necessary to untwist the deceptive cultural winds that batter the genders from all directions.

Let's understand that before a husband is a husband he is a man. He acts as a husband according to what he believes as a man. Before a wife is a wife she is a woman. She acts as a wife according to what she believes as a woman. Clarifying issues on male and female is paramount to clarifying issues as husband and wife.

So, first we're going to look at what God says about man and woman. Then, in the next chapter, we'll consider His Word about husbands and wives.

We've already established that genders were created by God. Consequently, men and women reflect the glory of God *equally*. Adam and Eve equally give us insight into the character of God. Adam's strength shows the strength of God. Eve's nurturing shows the nurturing of God. Which one is better? Neither. Both equally reveal truths about the character of the God of Creation. Therefore, there is no greater inherent value in being a man or a woman. None.

Being a man is not better than being a woman and being a woman is not better than being a man. Thoughts, words, or practices that demean one or the other do not come from God. God did not create one or the other and say, "That was a mistake." Every man should feel great that God made him man and every woman should feel great that God made her woman. God made them both after His image and His likeness.

Thankfully, God recorded stories of men and women in His Scripture through which we gain insight into what He intends for males and females. Those exalted in the Scripture are to be great gender role models. What does it mean to be a woman? Look to Rebecca, Jochebed, Rahab, Huldah, Anna, Sapphira, and others. What does it mean to be a man? Consider the lives of Abraham, Joseph, Gideon, Samuel, Hosea, Apollos, or Jude for starters. These are some of the lives God purposefully recorded for our benefit. When you read their lives, what do you see?

Rebecca's faithfulness to God's vision for her family directly impacted the history of an entire nation (Genesis 24–35). Jochebed defied a Pharaoh's orders, putting her life in harm's way for the survival of her son, Moses (Exodus 1–2). Her story also includes two Hebrew midwives, Shiphrah and Puah, who chose faithfulness to God over the government's law. Deborah was the only female judge of Israel in the period of the judges. She delivered Israel from the Canaanites when no man had the will to do so (Judges 4–5). Luke 8:1–3 mentions three women, Mary Magdalene, Joanna, and Susanna, among other women, who funded Jesus's ministry out of their private means.

These women are a small sample of whom God exalted as examples of biblical womanhood. Their lives teach us that God made woman with capacity for great faithfulness. A biblical woman is one who cultivates intimacy with the Father, Son, and Holy Spirit and trusts His will for her life.

What of the men? While Abraham is called the "Father of the faith" for laying the foundation of Israel, he also made significant mistakes in his journey (Genesis 11:27–25:11). David, a common shepherd boy, became well known for his military conquests but struggled mightily as a husband and father (1 Samuel 16:1–1, Kings 2:12, and 1 Chronicles 10:13–1; 29:30). Peter, an ordinary fisherman, was trained by Jesus to lead his kingdom but had a serious temper problem (Matthew 1:18–Acts 12:25 and 1 and 2 Peter). Paul was called out of the blindness of his religion to adoption in Christ and tasked with spreading the gospel from Jerusalem to Rome and beyond, but he was a murderer (Acts 9–Philemon).

God shows us through these men that man is capable of great faithfulness and great failure. A biblical man is one who deeply believes in the Father, Son, and Holy Spirit and faithfully follows God's will.

Jesus is, of course, the ultimate demonstration of life for all humanity. Because He is always the "easy" answer, I am looking to other men and women to add their contributions to the male/female reality. In all things, Jesus is phenomenal. However, that doesn't mean that looking to Rebecca or Abraham isn't helpful in understanding men and women.

Men should be proud to be men. Women should be proud to be women. Both are capable of great strength and eternal acts of faith. The strength and internal fortitude of a man or a woman does not come from being a man or a woman or from being married or single. Strength and internal fortitude come from believing in, and living faithfully to, the Father, Son, and Holy Spirit.

Being made male or female is the third of five pillars essential to who God has made you to be.

4. *We were made children of God.*
"From any tree of the garden you may eat freely; but from the tree of the knowledge of good and evil you shall not eat, for in the day that you eat from it you will surely die" (Genesis 2:16–17).

God gives Adam one stipulation concerning life in the garden of Eden: he cannot eat from the Tree of Knowledge of Good and Evil. The consequence of disobedience will be death. By death God does not mean nonexistence. Death, defined by God, is separation from the Father,

Son, and Holy Spirit family. As we saw in the last section, God exists as family: Father, Son, and Holy Spirit in perfect love. God made Adam and Eve in His image to be in His family. The essence of God's family is love and trust. Disobedience showed a lack of love. If Adam and Eve disobeyed, then they would be separated from the family.

Adam and Eve enjoyed all the benefits of being a son and a daughter. They were perfectly loved, perfectly provided for, and perfectly prepared. They lacked nothing.

To put this into a modern-day perspective, consider Julia Louis-Dreyfus, the well-known American actress most known as Elaine in the television comedy Seinfeld. Her family runs the French conglomerate Louis Dreyfus Group, which has experienced average annual gross sales in recent years exceeding $120 billion. Because she was born into the Louis Dreyfus family, she will inherit some portion of that estate.

How would you like to inherit that?

According to Scripture, as a child of God, you have an inheritance. 1 Peter 1:3–4 says,

> Blessed be the God and Father of our Lord Jesus Christ, who according to His great mercy has caused us to be born again to a living hope through the resurrection of Jesus Christ from the dead, to obtain an inheritance which is imperishable and undefiled and will not fade away, reserved in heaven for you.

God your Father has secured His inheritance for you. It is far more valuable than $120 billion. And it is yours, male or female. What kind of impact does that have on your life? How can you live in worry or fear? How can you be a victim? How can you be weak or needy? Where is pride? God has blessed both men and women by making them His sons and daughters, bestowing on each of them the glory of His inheritance.

Being made a child of God is the fourth of five essentials for knowing who God has designed you to be.

5. *You were made blessed.*
"God created man in His own image, in the image of God He created him; male and female He created them. *God blessed them*" (Genesis 1:27–28, emphasis added).

God made His children to be blessed. This makes sense, does it not? God is good and was not compelled in any way to create anything or anyone. So when He chose to create out of His goodness, He created children in His image and blessed them. According to Genesis 1:28, you were created for blessing and God is the One who blesses.

Blessing is a rich thread that runs through Scripture. When God chooses Abram to be the father of the nation of Israel, He says, "Go forth from your relative and from your father's house, to the land which I will show you; and I will make you a great nation, and I will bless you" (Genesis 12:1–2). Jesus opens His famous Sermon on the Mount by offering His blessing to eight different types of people. Paul begins his letter to the Ephesians, "Blessed be the God and Father of our Lord Jesus Christ, who has blessed us with every spiritual blessing in the heavenly places in Christ" (Ephesians 1:3). God made you to be blessed and He is the One who blesses you.

Many people are confused about the blessings of God. Some believe that God's blessings consist of money, houses, cars, and other material goods. Some believe that His blessings are physical health. Others believe that His blessings should be whatever they want them to be! And others are too busy pursuing their own blessings to care about God's.

Can God bless His people with material goods? Absolutely! Part of God's blessing for Adam and Eve was the abundant beauty and provision of the garden of Eden. Can God bless His people with physical health? Absolutely! The stories of Jesus's healings run through the Gospels. While God can bless in these ways, His foundational blessings are more substantive.

Paul lists six blessings after his opening comments in Ephesians 1. God blesses His people by:

1. Choosing them before the foundation of the world
2. Adopting them into His family
3. Redeeming them by forgiving their sins
4. Enlightening them by revealing His master plan to them
5. Endowing them with an inheritance
6. Sealing them in eternity by the Holy Spirit.

God blesses His people by joining Himself to them in a covenant relationship based on intimacy and faithfulness. He is not only the supreme blessor, He is the supreme blessing.

Unfortunately, many people become frustrated by their perception of God's lack of blessing. They have made the blessings more important than the blessor. What they can get (or feel they should get) from God has become more important than God Himself.

How many times have you seen relationships ruined when the gifts of the relationship become more important than the relationship itself? What is intended to be an act of generosity becomes an expectation and a disappointment.

Our Father is a master blessor. He knows how much you can handle that will not spoil your relationship with Him. He made you for blessing. And He is faithful to bless.

Made to be blessed is the final pillar of your identity.

Conclusion

Marital issues are intimately connected with not knowing who we are. To confront ourselves in marriage, we must discover who we really are.

You are:

- Designed in the image of God
- Made body and spirit,
- Created male or female
- Named son or daughter
- Blessed by God Himself

This is who God says you are and this is who God is perfecting in you! Let Him work! Let Him move! Like a master sculptor God is creating His eternal masterpiece in you. Rest in Him. Remind yourself daily of who you are in Him. Watch what happens in you when you forget. Return to Him and be still.

These are the foundational answers to the "Who am I?" question. This is the truth of God's Word and the reality of your design. This is living on the rock of Jesus. Can you imagine how you would feel about yourself if you embraced this? What would a marriage look like where both husband and wife embrace this truth and walk in it? Fantastic!

So why do we not experience this in our daily lives?

Why do we battle so hard against internal instability?

What is wrong with us?

CHAPTER 3
DIAGNOSE: KNOW YOUR SIN

You have issues. Your spouse or soon-to-be spouse has issues too, but you can't fix their issues. Your issues are so bad that the only remedy was the unjust crucifixion of the Son of God Himself. That's how messed up you are. You are not "kind of" messed up; you are fundamentally damaged. The glory and hope of the gospel is the present power of Jesus to heal and restore, lift and encourage, and bless and love in ways not humanly possible to heights not humanly attainable. But His restorative work must travel the corridors of our wounds and sins and pains and unbelief.

If you're not willing to accept that you need healing and correction, that you have deep, Christ-needing issues, then maybe you should get divorced now or choose to not marry and save your spouse or future spouse from years of unnecessary pain. Forget about marriage. In order for your life to work, you have to know *you*, understand the sickness *you* have, and learn how to overcome it.

The sickness you have is the reason why you struggle to experience God's design for your life. Your issues attack the very goodness and glory God created you for. Ignored, these issues will negatively affect your marriage. In fact, many issues in marriage are nothing more than undiagnosed or misdiagnosed *personal* issues.

Know your sin.
The keyword for this lesson is **diagnose**.

You've had health issues, car problems, and project difficulties where, for a variety of reasons, no one could figure out what was going on. Beyond frustrating. Being in a situation where you know there is something wrong but cannot figure out the cause is a difficult place to be. The difficulty will be more intense when your marriage is the place where something is wrong. Often times marriage challenges can be traced back to unresolved or improperly handled issues with one person. A husband or a wife is unaware of how their pasts, their relationships with God, or some other root is causing the strife in the marriage.

For the quality of our own lives and the quality of our marriages, we need to have our issues properly diagnosed. Life on the Rock is about allowing Jesus to minister to our wounds and empower us in our individual struggles. To deny His healing and His power is to live in our pain, forcing our spouses to unnecessarily endure our personal sin.

When the Good of the Garden Went Bad

God made all of creation, including Adam and Eve, in six days. At the end of each of the first five days God said, "It is good." At the end of the sixth day, the day in which He created Adam and Eve, Scripture says, "God saw all that He had made, and behold, it was very good" (Genesis 1:31).

God the Father, Son, and Holy Spirit existed in perfect harmony with the angels, man, and woman. All of creation worked in the beautiful way God had designed it to work.

So what went wrong?

God gave one prohibition to Adam: "The Lord God commanded man, saying, 'From any tree of the garden you may eat freely; but from the tree of the knowledge of good and evil you shall not eat, for in the day that you eat from it you will surely die" (Genesis 2:16–17). Adam and Eve were free to fully enjoy their relationship with the Father, Son, and Holy Spirit and everything the garden had to offer—except that one tree.

One day a provocateur showed up, a serpent craftier than any beast of the field. He questioned Eve about God's prohibition. He suggested that eating from the tree would not cause her death but would, in fact, make her special.

> When the woman saw that the tree was good for food, and that it was a delight to the eyes, and that the tree was desirable to make one wise, she took from its fruit and ate; and she gave also to her husband with her, and he ate. Then the eyes of both of them were opened, and they knew that they were naked; and they sewed fig leaves together and made themselves loin coverings (Genesis 3:6–7).

In an instant, the harmony of God's creation was wrecked. Adam and Eve disobeyed the One who had created and provided for them. The pristine reality, not just of the garden of Eden, but of the universe and of man himself, was shattered. Where Adam and Eve once had perfect peace with no issues, they were now, instantly, riddled with fear and guilt.

Biblically, fear and guilt are manifestations of the sickness of sin. Through Adam and Eve sin entered humanity. The internal peace and confidence they once had had fled. For the first time in their lives, Adam and Eve felt shame, guilt, fear, and anxiety.

Intimacy with God is marked by stability and strength. Sin rips man from holy intimacy with his Father. Left in the wake of sin was an insatiable instability that drove Adam and Eve to cover themselves and hide from God.

This is not what God intended. Man has been uniquely designed in all the universe for intimacy with the Father, Son, and Holy Spirit. Man's image of himself, his internal need for peace and stability, is *only* satisfied through intimacy with his Creator.

Because of the sin of Adam, all men and women, for all time, are born into an internal emptiness—the effect of being separated from God.

If we're going to successfully know our issues and properly diagnose ourselves so we can walk in freedom, we need to understand sin.

Categorize Your Sin to Diagnose Yourself

Four different categories of sin exist in the Bible:

1. *Original sin* refers to the sin of Adam and Eve in the garden of Eden. Every man and woman suffers from original sin.

2. *Generational sin* is passed on to us from our parents. Both original and generational sin are preexisting conditions: we're born with both.

3. *Personal sin* is what we do all on our own that has no direct connection to Adam or our family lines.

4. *Others' sin* stems from other people's sins that cause us harm.

We're going to work through each type of sin individually so that we can see how they sneak into and negatively affect our lives.

Original Sin and Women
After Adam and Eve disobeyed God, He cursed them individually. The curse He put on Eve is different than the curse He put on Adam. Therefore, men and women experience original sin differently.

Genesis 3:16 records the curse God put on Eve: "To the woman He said, 'I will greatly multiply your pain in childbirth, in pain you will bring forth children; Yet your desire will be for your husband, and he will rule over you.'"

God cursed Eve in two places: her role as mother and her role as wife. Every woman, everywhere, for all times, at the core of who she is, battles fear, insecurity, guilt, and instability in her role as a wife and a mother. This is not just a woman thing; this is an original sin thing.

First, God curses Eve in her role as mother. When God says, "I will greatly multiply your pain in childbirth, in pain you will bring forth children," He was not limiting the curse to the physical birthing process. The term "childbirth" refers to the entire mothering/nurturing role. Eve/women are going to struggle to be good mothers.

As an extension of the mothering role, women will also struggle with their homes. Because the home is where the mothering primarily happens, women battle with fear and insecurity about their homes. The home is never right when they place their trust in themselves or their husbands.

In addition to the role of mother, women suffer the curse of original sin in their roles as wives. The second part of the curse on women says, "Yet your desire will be for your husband, and he will rule over you."

Eve/women will have an unhealthy desire to be married. The pull on women to be married is deeply strong. The age differs in different cultures, but women seem to run a race to get married. In the United States, the current age appears to be thirty. If a woman is not married by thirty, she begins to fear the worst.

DIAGNOSE: KNOW YOUR SIN

One woman writes,

> The mark of Eve and the fear is so great that we let it over take us and sometimes in the dating world, we don't make very good decisions on picking a partner because we let that fear cloud our judgment. I have a girlfriend who was 32 at the time and she loved the Lord and was seeking the Lord. She really wanted to find a strong man of God and settle down and get married. However she continued to date men that did not treat her well and who were against everything she believed in and yet she knowingly continued to settle. I have a cousin who is 37, divorced, and a single mom and on the outside she is the funniest and "happiest" person but deep down I know she is scared to death of not finding another man. Her exact words to me almost every time we talk is "I am so afraid that nobody will want a single mom at this age and I'm scared to be alone forever."

Once a woman is married, the curse of Eve manifests itself in the woman's desire to control her husband. God says, "Yet your desire will be for your husband, and *he will rule over you*" (Genesis 3:16, emphasis added). The curse of Eve pits wife against husband in seeking leadership of the family. Nothing a husband ever does is good enough, in time enough, or done in the right way.

Because these are the marks of Eve, all women everywhere suffer them. Misdiagnosed, these realities will be accepted as "normal" and "just part of being a woman." Women may make horrific decisions in their love lives, hound their husbands at home, press hard into their children, and experience no rest in life. They will try all sorts of remedies—medications, alcohol, exercise, working harder, quitting, surgery, getting a new husband, buying a bigger house—to satisfy what they feel inside. None of it will work. The mark of Eve is a matter of sin that can only be, and can easily be, remedied through the love of the Father, Son, and Holy Spirit. At the end of this chapter we will see how the resurrection of Jesus can heal every woman from the effects of Eve.

Original Sin and Men
God curses Adam in Genesis 3:17–19 saying,

> Then to Adam He said, "Because you have listened to the voice of your wife, and have eaten from the tree about which I commanded you, saying, 'You shall not eat from it'; Cursed is the ground because of you; In toil you will eat of it all the days of your life. Both thorns and thistles it shall grow for you; And you will eat the plants of the field; By the sweat of your face You will eat bread, Till you return to the ground, Because from it you were taken; For you are dust, And to dust you shall return."

First, this is not a blanket indictment on men ever listening to their wives. However, it is an indictment against Adam for not standing up to his wife and obeying God's word. Adam was derelict as a son of God because he followed his wife's disobedience.

Consequently, all men are born with the sin of Adam. The sin of Adam strikes men primarily in the areas of provision and significance. All men battle fear in not having enough money to provide for themselves and their family, and all men battle fear and insecurity in whether or not their lives matter.

God says, "Cursed is the ground because of you." Adam's sin changed ecology. The ground no longer works the way God originally intended it to work because of Adam. Just as childbirth for the woman means the whole enterprise of motherhood, so too does the ground refer to all of man's efforts as a producer. Man is to produce. However, everywhere he tries to produce is cursed.

Therefore, man will toil. He will have frustrating work and frustrated productivity all the days of his life. He will live in fear, insecurity, and guilt as a producer. Furthermore, his productivity will produce "thorns and thistles." The result of his work will always be impure. By the sweat of his face—again a reference to the amount of work a man has to do to produce—he will eat plants and bread.

Men daily battle against the fear of failure and disappointment as producers. We live under constant financial pressure. Notice in Adam's curse the frequency of eating. Four times God expresses how much men will struggle with providing for food. Men fear not having enough to eat. Consequently, men have a lightning-fast calculator in their minds that totals up the cost of everything their wives want to do in their homes. And the fighting begins!

Furthermore, men live exhausted because of how much they have to work to produce whatever it is they can get. Work frustration leaves men with little left for their wives and families. When men are with their wives, they may not be fully present because their minds are on work.

Satisfaction for a man comes from his production. If he perceives he is producing well, he will be in a better emotional condition. If he thinks he is failing or slipping, he will be affected emotionally. A man's emotions are tied to his productivity.

It should be no surprise then that a man loves efficiency. The more efficient something is the more it produces. The more it produces the more men don't have to fear not having. The less fear men have the more joy men can have.

This is why men want to fix women's problems.
This is why men can be so absent.
This is why money is such a major issue for men.
This is why men are so single-minded and focused and don't do well with distractions.

Unfortunately, God was not done cursing man. After cursing the ground and its implications, God says, "By the sweat of your face You will eat bread, Till you return to the ground, Because from it you were taken; For you are dust, And to dust you shall return" (Genesis 3:19).

Man is going to return to the ground because from the ground man was taken. No matter how great man's accomplishments are he is going to die and go back to where he came from. With the ultimate ax laid to the root of every man's pride, God shouts to Adam and to all men, "*You are dust*, and to dust you shall return" (emphasis added).

Man has been struck in his desire to accomplish great works in his life. Man will spend his days in futility to build a life that means something so others will look at him and think he's successful. At the end of all his years he will lay down and die. He will be buried in the ground and his corpse will erode to dust—the same dust from which he was created. No book captures the plight of man and the curse of Adam better than Ecclesiastes. The entire book could be retitled, "The Consequences of Life in Adam." One sample of Solomon's Adamic observations is found in Ecclesiastes 2:21–23:

> When there is a man who has labored with wisdom, knowledge and skill, then he gives his legacy to one who has not labored with them. This too is vanity and a great evil. For what does a man get in all his labor and in his striving with which he labors under the sun? Because all his days his task is painful and grievous; even at night his mind does not rest. This too is vanity.

Because of this facet of Adam's curse, all men run a three-stage race:

1. In the first stage man says, "I can do anything," and he busies himself trying to prove to himself and to others that he can.

2. In the second stage man asks, "Does anything I've done really matter?" He begins to question all the time and resources he's burned. What has he really done?

3. In the final stage, man is confronted with the question, "What do I have to leave behind?" Men live with a profound fear of insignificance. This drives men. There is no rest, no joy, no substance, and very little room for anything else.

In addition to men's financial calculators, they also have accomplishment clocks. If what you want to discuss doesn't factor into helping men continue to climb whatever hill they're on, then they often have very little time for it. So men are short, curt, and can be seen as rude.

This is the disease of original sin as it affects women and men. You need to understand how powerful the force of original sin is in your life. Ask the Lord to show you how the sins of Adam and Eve are driving your motives, your tone, and your actions. The result should be insight into yourself and great compassion for your spouse as you begin to understand the depths of what they're dealing with as well. Hopefully you can begin to move to common ground in your mutual fight against original sin at work in both of you.

Generational Sin

Unfortunately, the disease of sin does not stop with original sin. Generational sin is the second layer of the sickness we have inside us. Like original sin, generational sin is a preexisting condition we are born into. Generational sin refers to your patterns of sin that were passed down from your mother and father that are not original sin. While original sin is certainly generational, there are sin patterns you have inherited that are not directly related to the consequences on Adam and Eve but are specific to your family line.

Biblically, we see a clear example of generational sin in the lineage of Jesse and David. In 1 Samuel 16, the prophet Samuel is directed by God to go to the house of Jesse to anoint the next king of Israel. The current king, Saul, has failed in his faithfulness to the Lord. When

Samuel finds Jesse, he learns that Jesse has seven children. Contrary to physical appearances and cultural customs, Samuel anoints the youngest son, David, as Israel's next king.

Later in his life, David fulfills Samuel's anointing and becomes King. Second Samuel 3:1–5, 14 records that David had seven wives. This does not include Bathsheba, who would later become his wife whose first husband, Uriah, David had murdered. While David's polygamy[5] was never directly confronted by God, the consequences of his sin are seen in the collapse of his family. David's oldest son, Amnon, raped his half-sister, Tamar. When David did not intervene, her full brother, Absalom, did, and set into motion a plan that ultimately killed his sister's rapist (2 Samuel 13:23–39).

What is relevant in our understanding of generational sin is that there is no indication given that Jesse, David's father, had any sexual indiscretions in his life. David did not inherit any sexual issues from his family, but he certainly had such issues.

Solomon was born to David's eighth wife, Bathsheba. He was raised in a family where multiple wives were acceptable, and his father killed his mother's first husband. Solomon took David's sin two steps further. Solomon married many foreign women. While David was a polygamist, all of his wives were Israelites. Solomon, however, married many women who worshipped different gods.

---

[5] In the time of David, polygamy was accepted for several reasons. For one, women did not have the economic opportunities they have today. Without a husband, a woman was left to prostitute or to live off of their fathers or brothers. Polygamy became a way to keep women from destitution. Additionally, polygamy was used as a way to form political alliances.

First Kings 11:1–2 says, "Now King Solomon loved many foreign women along with the daughter of Pharaoh, Moabite, Ammonite, Edomite, Sidonian, and Hittite women, from the nations concerning which the Lord has said to the sons of Israel, 'You shall not associate with them, nor shall they associate with you, for they will surely turn your heart away after their gods.' Solomon held fast to these in love."

The second step Solomon took in advancing his father's polygamy was idolatry. He set up idols in Israel worshiping the gods of the foreign women he married. Because of his sin, Israel was now filled with statues and altars to gods of all the surrounding people.

As the son of Naamah the Ammonite and King Solomon, Rehoboam was born into a family where polygamy and idolatry were regularly practiced. He followed in his father's idolatrous ways. Rehoboam's son Abijam did the same.

Solomon, Rehoboam, and Abijam were born into the generational sin of polygamy and idolatry. These were preexisting conditions they did not deal with in their lives.

In a fascinating turn, Abijam's son Asa turned in a different direction. He stood against the generational sin he was born into and lived a far different life. We will look at what he did at the end of this chapter.

What about you?

What are the generational sins you were born into?

As you consider the issues you deal with, how many of them can easily be found in your lineage?

- Anger
- Anxiety
- Depression
- Suicide
- Idolatry
- Witchcraft
- Obesity
- Rebellion
- Divorce
- Fear

This is not an exhaustive list but hopefully serves as a way to stir up your mind to some areas you may be battling that you have inherited.

Without an understanding of generational sin, it's easy to take out these issues on a spouse. Because it's been a part of your family line for a long time, generational sin can be written off as something you've had your whole life: "This is just who I am." However, the great truth in the Lord is that you no longer have to be bound by these things.

Personal Sin

The third category of sin is personal sin: those that you come up with on your own. They are not attributed to original sin or generational sin. For example, no one in your family line has ever struggled with gambling but you picked it up, and now it's controlling you and destroying your life.

Adam and Eve's fall in the garden is certainly the first example of personal sin. They did not learn that from anyone nor was it passed to them from their parents. Remember what their sin was: they were guilty of wanting more than what God had for them. They sinned because they were not satisfied with God's provision.

We see another example of personal sin in Genesis 4 in the life of Cain, Adam and Eve's son. A time came for Cain and his brother, Abel, to give an offering to the Lord. Cain gave an offering from the ground; Abel gave from his flock. God had regard for Abel's offering but not for Cain's. Cain became angry.

God appeared to Cain and said, "If you do well, will not your countenance be lifted up? And if you do not do well, sin is crouching at the door; and its desire is for you, but you must master it" (Genesis 4:7). Cain failed. He did not master his sin. His sin mastered him and he killed his brother.

The issue in the relationship between Cain and Abel was not Abel's issue, or both Cain and Abel's issue. The issue was only Cain's. He did not deal with his personal sin and it cost Abel's life.

But notice also that, according to God, Cain not only had the responsibility, but the ability, to deal with his issue. As we have stated before, many marital issues are unresolved personal issues.

In addition to these early Genesis examples of personal sins, Jesus regularly dealt with the topic. Here is a list of some of the sins Jesus confronts in His Sermon on the Mount in Matthew 5–7:

DIAGNOSE: KNOW YOUR SIN

- Prejudice
- Anger
- Sexual immorality/adultery
- Divorce
- Breaking your word
- Getting back at others
- Arrogant giving
- Materialism
- Anxiety
- Judgmentalism
- Loving God and money
- Praying that draws attention to yourself

Jesus taught against personal sin. He called His followers to personal responsibility and ability. He endured the cross to free individuals from their bondage to their sin. That is His work, His role, and His joy.

Unfortunately, many do not want to admit their sin. Consider the man who was sexually active before he got married. In his sexual promiscuity he did things that brought him great pleasure and gave him distinct memories. Now married, the man is angry because his wife will not do those things. He lives unsatisfied and blames her when, in fact, the issue is with him. In a similar situation, a sexually active man now lives in shame and guilt because of his sexual past. His marriage suffers because he does not want any physical contact. The wife feels unloved and unwanted.

In a different situation, a woman spends time on Facebook. She sees post after post of friends traveling to different places and other friends enjoying great restaurants. Jealousy builds. She begins to pressure her husband to have the kind of life she sees her friends having. The wife resents her husband because their lives do not measure up to what she sees on Facebook. She blames him. However, the issue is hers, not his.

Personal sin is a devastating source of individual pain and marital conflict.

Others' Sin

The final category of sin is others' sin, which comes from the abuse or neglect done to us by other people. The degree of others' sin can vary from simple disappointment of a broken promise to the severity of physical and emotional abuse. Others' sin can be verbal—"You're good for nothing"—to non-verbal: no physical contact and no physical contact.

It's a sad reality that many of us have suffered through horrendous personal attacks at the hands of others.

Scripture does not hide from the evil of men. But, Scripture also shows the powerful hand of God to overcome evil regardless of what man does.

We briefly looked at Joseph's story in Chapter 1. Here we look at more detail. Joseph's story is a powerful narrative of God working in the life of a person victimized by others. Joseph's mom died when he was a little boy. He was born into a dysfunctional family with eleven brothers born by four different women. When he was a boy, Joseph received a vision from God that one day his brothers would bow down to him. As a little brother would do, he ran and bragged to his brothers about his dream.

His oldest brothers were so incensed that they threw him into a pit he couldn't get out of. Now, if this was all they did the act could be chalked up to one of those things older brothers do to younger brothers. However, the older brothers went much further.

A nomadic group of people were traveling nearby. The brothers decided to sell their youngest brother into slavery and stage a fake murder scene so that their father would believe Joseph was dead. Imagine Joseph's fear as a teenager being led to a cage in that nomadic caravan. Maybe he thought the joke would end and his brothers would come to his rescue. At some point that caravan went over the horizon, Joseph lost sight of his brothers, and the harsh reality of his life set in.

He ended up in Egypt. While in Egypt he worked in the house of a man named Potiphar. Potiphar's wife liked Joseph and wanted to have sex with him. Joseph fled. Potiphar's wife lied and accused Joseph of trying to rape her. He went to jail. Through an amazing turn of events, Joseph ended up, after years in prison, in front of the Pharaoh. The leader of Egypt had a dream no one could interpret. But God was with Joseph, and He had been the whole time. Joseph interpreted Pharaoh's dream so Pharaoh made him the Number Two man in all the Egyptian empire.

Because of a famine in the land of Joseph's brothers, they travel to Egypt to find grain. Little do they know that Joseph is now in charge of grain distribution. Upon revealing himself to his brothers, they begin to fear that Joseph is going to take revenge and have them killed. In this incredible scene, Joseph utters one of the most famous lines in the Bible: "As for you, you meant evil against me, but God meant it for good in order to bring about this present result, to preserve many people alive" (Genesis 50:20).

The trajectory of Joseph's entire life was changed because of the sin of his brothers. What they did to him was horrific. He was further victimized by Potiphar's wife's false accusation of rape. Yet, Joseph knew God was faithful. He fulfilled Joseph's vision: his brothers did bow down to him.

Joseph's life teaches us that God is faithful. No one has to allow the sin of others to define their lives. Joseph could have very easily played the victim and lived a life in the shadows, complaining, defeated, and despondent. But no—although he was severely victimized, he was not a victim. Furthermore, God used the very evil his brothers committed to propel Joseph to a position of power where he would be used to rescue and help thousands. God is a master at what He does.

Many of us continue to suffer others' sins unnecessarily. No doubt what many of you have endured would be difficult to even hear about. I've heard some unbelievable stories of abuse, neglect, and abandonment. But those things do not have to define you. And none of them have to stop you from walking in the fullness of what God has for you.

Be sober-minded in your marriage. Are you taking out the abuse and neglect of others on your spouse? If so, seek out the help you need. Go to your spouse, confess, and ask them to walk with you on a journey of healing. You do not have to be a victim. You do not have to suffer unnecessarily. You do not have to take out your pain on your spouse.

The Role of the Holy Spirit as Diagnostician

Thankfully, we are not left to ourselves to understand the different ways we are afflicted by the disease of sin. The Holy Spirit has been given to us as the person of God responsible for our healing and empowerment.

After spending three and a half years with His disciples, and days before His crucifixion, Jesus prepared His men for life when He was gone. He makes a remarkable statement in John 16:7, "But I tell you the truth, it is to your advantage that I go away, for if I do not go away, the Helper (the Holy Spirit) will not come to you; but if I go, I will send Him to you." Jesus just said it will be better for the disciples if He leaves! How is that possible? Because the Helper is coming and the Helper's ministry will be better for the disciples than Jesus' was. Staggering.

One of the many ministries of the Holy Spirit is the work of transforming us into the image of Jesus that we were originally created to be. The Apostle Paul explains this in 2 Corinthians 3:18, "But we all, with unveiled face, beholding as in a mirror the glory of the Lord, are being transformed into the same image from glory to glory, just as from the Lord, the Spirit." In other words, the life of Jesus gave way to the ministry of the Spirit whose work is to heal us of sin and empower us for life as He shapes us into God's image.

The Holy Spirit carries out His transformational work in our lives by revealing to us various ways in which sin has been, and is, afflicting our lives. We do not have to figure out our issues on our own. We can ask the Lord to reveal them to us. And we can ask with confidence knowing that His ministry of healing, restoration, and power will be carried out with love.

Conclusion

Marital algebra states that 1+1=1. The healthiness of each "1" has direct impact on the healthiness of the combined "1." To be godly spouses we must first be godly people. To be godly people we need to know ourselves and be properly diagnosed. A proper diagnosis will keep us from putting new tires on a car that needs oil.

As we grow in the understanding of our sickness, we can help our spouses learn how to navigate us better. We should not get mad because someone else cannot figure us out when we cannot figure ourselves out!

Get to know yourself. Know how God has designed you. Be open to learning how the sickness of sin is affecting you. Original, generational, personal, and others' sins are powerful sources of instability that you will take out on your spouse if you do not deal with them. Ask the Holy Spirit to show you how sin is affecting you in ways you cannot see. Take ownership of your life. Where you have sin, confess it, ask forgiveness, receive forgiveness, and move forward. Allow the Spirit to teach you how to deal with your own sin in the love, mercy, grace, and power of Jesus. You will feel your life on the Rock become steady and your heart become increasingly secure. Instead of your spouse enduring the vibrations of your sin, they will enjoy the pleasures of your faith.

CHAPTER 4
RELAX: APPLY THE SECRET INGREDIENT

I have known Mike since 2001. He has become a great friend and brother in the Lord. Our families are super close and we have traveled everywhere together. He is reputed to have an incredible pancake recipe. I grew up on my dad's pancakes and have worked hard since my kids were born to perfect my own pancake recipe. I think what I have is pretty special and tastes fantastic. However, my kids continually say Mike's are better!

At a men's retreat, Mike made his pancakes. I finally got to see what he does!

I asked Mike, "What do you put in your pancakes?"

He replied, "Two cups of flour, baking soda, eggs, milk . . . and one cup of sugar."

"One cup of sugar? No wonder my kids think your pancakes are better than mine. That's cheating!"

Mike had a secret ingredient that affected the whole taste of his pancakes. His secret ingredient was not a dash of cinnamon or a little bit of vanilla—his secret ingredient was a cup of sugar.

There is a secret ingredient to life and marriage. Our Father makes a particular reality available to us that drastically changes the flavor of our lives and consequently drastically changes the flavor of our marriages.

God's secret ingredient is grace.

Sin is the contagion that corrupts and destroys. Grace is the burst of light that brings life and breath and relief. Grace is the overwhelming phenomenon of the Holy God initiating restoration and forgiveness to any who will come to Him. Sin is utterly discouraging. If you are not discouraged by your sin, you are not being honest about your sin. Grace is amazingly encouraging. Breath-by-breath living in grace continually liberates the soul and elevates any person to deep connectedness with the Father, Son, and Holy Spirit.

The beneficial impact of grace on life and marriage is incalculable.

Walk in grace.
The keyword in this lesson is **relax**.

We are tightly wound people. Living under the tyranny of performance, having to do everything on your own, will make you tight. The grace of our Father lays an axe to the root of performance living, giving birth to fearless love that we can relax in and trust.

The Biblical Significance of Grace

I want to convince you of the weight that our Father intends grace to have in our lives and marriages by working through some texts in the New Testament before we break down grace in the garden.

Consider the way John describes Jesus in John 1:14–16: "And the Word became flesh, and dwelt among us, and we saw His glory, glory as of the only begotten from the Father, full of grace and truth. John testified about Him and cried out, saying, 'This was He of whom I said, "He who comes after me has a higher rank than I, for He existed before me."' For of His fullness we have all received, and grace upon grace."

According to John, when we see Jesus we see grace. Grace and truth are two of the revelatory characteristics of the Incarnate Son of God. And then John writes that receiving the fullness of Jesus can be described as having received "grace upon grace." Grace is what I see when I see Jesus and grace is what I receive when I receive Jesus.

Grace is not ancillary or tangential; grace is center and pervasive.

The Apostle Paul wrote thirteen of the twenty-seven New Testament letters. Paul begins and ends every one of his letters with a commendation toward grace. So he begins 1 Corinthians saying, "Grace to you and peace from God our Father and the Lord Jesus Christ" (1 Corinthians 1:3). He ends 1 Corinthians, "The grace of the Lord Jesus be with you. My love be with you all in Christ Jesus. Amen" (1 Corinthians 16:23–24). Therefore, every one of Paul's letters is a grace sandwich filled with supernatural truth further explaining grace. Peter opens his two letters with similar greetings to Paul's.

And then there is the book of Revelation, the last book of the Bible. What began in Genesis 1:1 with, "In the beginning, God created the heavens and the earth," ends with the last verse in Revelation. For 1,500 years, on three different continents, in three different languages, by over forty men, God, through the Holy Spirit, has orchestrated the authorship of His Sacred Text. The last verse of Revelation closes the inspired book. What are the closing words that God chose to leave us with in Revelation 22:21?

"The grace of the lord Jesus be with all. Amen."

Grace is the secret sauce of life and marriage.

The Personal Significance of Grace

My daughter, Claire, is in elementary school. An outbreak of lice once hit her friends. We were concerned because Claire had been at the same sleepover with several of the girls who eventually got lice. We took her to a lady who specializes in combing lice out of hair. When we got to her office, one of Claire's friends was already there getting the lice removed. I watched as the lady meticulously removed each louse and nit. She had a bright light that circled a large magnifying glass that she pressed closely to the girl's hair. The process took four hours!

We often use the same degree of scrutiny to comb through our lives that the nitpicker used to comb through the girl's hair. We are professionals at picking apart our lives one molecule at a time. Nothing we do is good enough or right enough. We are never the right shape or have the right amount of money in the bank. We scrutinize how we perform in business meetings and social settings and then shred ourselves from any mistakes we perceived we made. This is another wonderful consequence of the sickness of our sin.

Of course, we have come to this behavior honestly. Our parents fought the same fight. They criticized themselves and beat themselves up long before we did.

And then there is our culture. The United States seems to be built on a culture of tearing down. Jealousy, judgmentalism, gossip, finger-pointing, anger, and much more are everywhere.

Criticism begets criticism. Scrutiny begets scrutiny.

This spills over into our relationships in general and our marriages in particular. We treat others the same way we treat ourselves. This makes sense because you cannot treat someone with something you don't have or don't regularly practice. So the same critical spirit we live out of is the same spirit in which we treat our spouses and our kids.

We need to get this so that we can appreciate grace. But further than that, we need to appreciate our current condition so that we can see the difficulty in changing and so that we can see what Jesus wants to change.

Coming to faith in Jesus is far more than having your sins forgiven. At least it is in the way many of us have come to define having our sins forgiven. Sadly, most of us live as if having our sins forgiven means I no longer cuss, look at porn, or do drugs. As long as I do not do that and go to church every so often, I am good!

Argh.

Walking with Christ, being born again into the Kingdom of God, and being seated at the right hand of the God of the universe is so much more. Jesus wants to change us. He wants to change how we see and understand life. He wants to change how we deal with issues. He wants to change how we relate with God. He wants to change our past, present, and future. And He wants to change how we treat ourselves!

He wants to transform us from people who reflexively tear down ourselves to those who treat ourselves with the same grace our Father treats us with. In fact, according to the passages we have already looked at, we can decidedly say that our Father's preferred disposition towards us is grace. Grace is the tone and rhythm of God's relationship with us.

Our desperate need is to live in and out of the grace that the Father, Son, and Holy Spirit work together to provide.

Choosing the Shame of Fig Leaves Over the Grace of Leather

Adam and Eve's response to their sin gives us a paradigm of what life looks like when we do not live by grace. God's response to their sin shows us the contrast of grace. In Genesis 3, this contrast can be described as the difference between choosing fig leaves or leather.

As the story goes, God put Adam in the garden of Eden and told him that he could eat from any tree of the garden—except the Tree of Knowledge of Good and Evil. Unfortunately, Adam and Eve fall in temptation and do exactly what God told them not to do. Immediately at the moment they ate, something *inside* of them changed. They *felt* differently. Genesis 3:7a says, "Then the eyes of both of them were opened and they knew that they were naked." Before they had eaten, they had experienced their nudity in the purity of God. After they had eaten, their experience changed. Where they once lived in innocence, now they lived in guilt and shame. Where they once knew stability, now they lived in instability. We are going to track how fig-leaf living affects their individual instability and the instability in their marriage.

This is evidenced by what they do next: "Then the eyes of both of them were opened and they knew that they were naked; and they sewed fig leaves together and made themselves loin coverings" (Genesis 3:7). Adam and Eve acted on their own to deal with their own issue. They made fig leaves and covered their nakedness.

Problem solved!

Nope.

In verse 8 God comes to see them. Even though they have covered themselves with fig leaves, when Adam and Eve hear God approaching, they hide! The fig leaves have done little. While they are physically covered, they still feel guilt and shame. Add fear to their guilt and shame because now they're hiding.

Their problems increase.

God calls out, asking where they are. The man replies, "I heard the sound of You in the garden, and I was afraid because I was naked; so I hid myself" (Genesis 3:10). Adam was covered but still dealing with powerful, internal instability.

God asks him how he knows he is naked. Did Adam eat from the tree he was told not to eat from? In one of the great lines of Scripture for its accurate portrayal of what fig-leaf living does, Adam says, "The woman whom you gave to be with me, she gave me from the tree, and I ate" (Genesis 3:12). Now, in addition to guilt, shame, and fear, you can add denial and blame. Can you see the kind of life that fig-leaf living leads to?

There is no amount of sophistication or high quality fig-leaf living that can deliver anyone from the internal instability that plagues the soul. None. It does not work. And, when rightly understood, fig-leaf living is ridiculous.

Imagine you have a great friend that you love and have known a long time. You have walked through life together and truly enjoy each other. One day they walk up to you and punch you in the face. They hit you cleanly and hard. You are bewildered and blindsided. What is going on? You feel rejected, angry, and betrayed. To remedy the situation, your friend goes to the local super-cool fashion store and buys a nice pair of jeans *for themselves*. And this is supposed to fix the issue between the two of you!

Insanity.
That doesn't make any sense.

But that is exactly what Adam and Eve did. They offended God. They sinned against Him and broke their relationship with Him. Adam and Eve's solution was to make themselves clothes! *Clothes*. Yet we are all guilty of doing the same thing.

Let's diagnose this properly.

The Problem of Fig-Leaf Living

Because of their sin, Adam and Eve suffered sin's symptoms through shame, guilt, fear, denial, and blame. Their condition changed from closeness to God to separation from their Father. What they once had in abundance—intimacy—they now lacked severely. After the fall, they had only one treatment option: forgiveness.

You have to see the connection between their instability and their sin. Sin is the root cause of what they are feeling internally.

Fig leaves do nothing for their instability—at all. And their fig-leaf living leads to division in their marriage. Adam is denying his role and pointing fingers at his wife. Do they need to go to couples counseling and learn how to be better communicators? No. They need to learn how to live in grace, deal with root issues, and receive forgiveness from God.

There are terrible downsides to fig-leaf living. In the first place, this way of life completely cuts the Father, Son, and Holy Spirit out of life. Where is the Lord in what Adam is doing? Nowhere. Well, without the Lord man is left to live on his own. On his own, man bears all the responsibility of life and all the pressure that comes with it. If man does not come through, then nothing is ever going to happen.

When anyone cuts out God, life now depends on them and on how they perform. Therefore, they begin scrutinizing everything they do! Nothing is good enough or right enough. Life is lived full of fear because no one else is there to carry the weight.

This does not only happen when a person cuts God out of their whole life; it also happens when you cut out God from a specific area of your life. If you asked Adam while he was hiding, "Do you believe in God? Do you think He is good in all things?" Certainly Adam would have said, "Yes." Nevertheless, he had an area of his life that he was not taking to the Lord. You do not have to abandon God totally to live with fig leaves; you just have to withhold specific areas from Him. In this condition a person will carry that scrutiny into their other relationships and their marriage. A spouse may be able to survive that, but it will be a lifelong, excruciating marathon of garbage.

Secondly, fig-leaf living rejects the character of God. Adam is not getting the benefit of God's grace and mercy. Man presupposes God is going to smite him off the face of the earth. He is hiding. (The picture of Adam hiding from God behind a bush is quite an interesting sight!) Now man suffers unnecessarily and exacerbates his condition.

Fig-leaf living always leads to men and women walking apart from God in the full weight of the pressure of their performance. Nothing is ever good enough. When issues come up, the claws come out: denial, rage, anger, and on.

Grace is not given because grace is not received. One generation of fig-leaf living begets another as moms and dads unknowingly model for their children a life of scrutiny, criticism, and self-destruction.

So what does grace look like?
How does God deal with Adam and Eve's issues?

The Solution of Forgiveness

Grace refers to the entire disposition of the Father, Son, and Holy Spirit to bless creation and the created. God was not compelled or coerced to make creation or to make man. Our Father did so as an act of grace to bless a people with the experience of fellowship with Him!

- In the beginning, God made man and woman and "God blessed them" (Genesis 1:28).

- Jesus opened His sermon on the mount with nine statements of blessing (Matthew 5:1–11).

- Paul writes that we experience God's grace in the spiritual blessings of being chosen, adopted, redeemed, enlightened, and sealed by the Holy Spirit (Ephesians 1:1–14).

- The Holy Spirit graces us with gifts to be used in kingdom work (1 Corinthians 12).

- Peter writes that God has, by grace, "granted to us His precious and magnificent promises" (2 Peter 1:4).

We also experience God's grace in the way He deals with sins. Confronted with the sin of Adam and Eve, God moves quickly to deal with the issue and restore intimacy. Notice, even though God is the one offended, He is the one who initiates restoration! Our Father does not wait to see who goes first.

God's first step in the grace of forgiveness is to punish the sin. He marks Adam and Eve with the curses we worked through in the last chapter. He does not allow them to hide. He does not delay in dealing with the issue. He does not minimize or trivialize what they have done. But, He also does not yell at them, He does not condemn them, and He does not belittle them. His punishment maintains the dignity of Adam and Eve by holding them accountable as mature, capable persons.

However, their punishment does not fit the crime. When God put Adam in the garden of Eden, He told Adam that if he sinned he would "surely die" (Genesis 2:17). Another reason fig-leaf living does not work is that it diminishes the severity of sin. Sin is a matter of life and death. Where there is sin there is, by necessity, death.

So, the second step of God's restoration was to provide a substitute. Somebody had to die. Sin carries a sentence of condemnation. However, God was unwilling to condemn His children. A substitute was needed. Genesis 3:21 says, "The Lord God made garments of skin for Adam and his wife, and clothed them." God substituted the lives of two animals. The animals received Adam and Eve's condemnation. While not completely satisfying God's requirement, the substitution of the animals meant that God would not condemn His children. Instead of condemning Adam and Eve, God condemned the two animals.

Furthermore, God's substitution also meant that intimacy with Adam and Eve was restored. The issues between them were healed. Brokenness was mended. There were no grudges, no secret storing of anger, and no baggage to carry. But God's work of restoration was not done.

The third step in God's grace was to make necessary changes. In Genesis 3:22–24 we find out that God drives Adam and Eve out of the garden of Eden and closes the entrance with an angel and a flaming sword. Grace does not mean the relationship has to continue in the state it was in. Grace makes the necessary changes to the relationship that promote health and intimacy.

God closes off the garden so that Adam and Eve would not eat from the Tree of Life and live in this animal-skin-covered condition forever. God had other plans for the relationship and their sin required a change. The change afforded Adam and Eve continued intimacy with their Father and continued blessings. The fruitfulness of their post-garden life is seen in Genesis 4:1: Adam and Eve give birth to their firstborn, Cain.

Grace did not mean God dismissed their sin. Grace did not mean the relationship had to change. In grace, God acted to confront the root issues, restore intimacy, and make the changes necessary so that the relationship could continue.

Fig-leaf living left Adam and Eve hiding in a bush, unstable.

Leather-living left Adam and Eve intimate with the Lord, stable, and experiencing His blessing for their lives.

The Sufficiency of the Cross Reveals Ultimate Grace

If you are a follower of Jesus, then you already believe that Jesus died on the cross for the forgiveness of our sins and was resurrected so that we can have life. You know that God's sacrifice of the two animals in the garden of Eden foreshadows the ultimate grace God provided by sacrificing His Son on the cross. Walking and living in grace is just embracing the fullness of the cross.

The cross means that God your Father initiated and initiates restoration. He is not waiting for you to make the first move even though you are the one who is guilty. "In this is love, not that we loved God, but that He loved us and sent His Son to be the propitiation for our sins" (1 John 4:10). The cross means that God loves you and initiated restoration by sacrificing His Son for your sin. Whatever your perception is of your Father, let it be tested by the cross. Through the cross your Father cries out, "Come to Me and let me deal with your sin."

And, the cross means that Jesus's beating is sufficient for your life. Quit beating yourself up. Your sins are the reason why Jesus was beaten. Jesus did not get beat up so that you could beat up yourself! Hebrews 10:10 says, "By this will (the will of our Father) we have been sanctified through the offering of the body of Jesus Christ once for all." Your Father provided you the ultimate grace by condemning sin in Jesus once for all. Now, today, "There is no condemnation for those who are in Christ Jesus" (Romans 8:1).

One day I had sinned against the Lord. I brought my mess before Him and confessed. He forgave me, and then I heard Him say, "Son, do not ever bring this up with me again." He wanted me to know that once I ask forgiveness and receive it, the matter is over. I am not to continue to dwell on it.

This is grace.

Leave Your Leaves

My kids are old enough to dress themselves but they don't know *how* to dress themselves! So getting dressed can become a war between whatever mismatched, picked-up-off-the-floor ensemble they put together and the clean, matched clothes my wife and I want them to wear. (We are ready for them to get to the age where it just does not matter and we can let them wear whatever.) Invariably we win and our kids at least have matching socks.

So what will it be for you: Will you continue to dress yourself in leaves or let God dress you in leather? Three things happen when you let God dress you:

First, He is going to confront your root sins. He is going to make known to you the issues you are guilty of. He is going to maintain your dignity by holding you accountable for what you are guilty of. God is perfectly aware of what your spouse, or anyone else, has done. In grace-living we are vulnerable to the Lord and allow Him to show *us* what *we* have done.

Second, He is not going to condemn you! Grace deals with issues without condemnation. When you make mistakes, when you sin against our Father *and bring your sin to Him*, you will receive none of the following:

- Condemnation
- Ripping
- Yelling
- Silent treatment
- Delay
- Piling on

None of these are the way our Father treats His children. He is the perfect parent and perfectly models how to deal with issues. He will hold you accountable for your sin but He will not cut you out of the family. "My son, do not reject the discipline of the Lord or loathe His reproof, for whom the Lord loves He reproves, even as a father corrects the son in whom he delights" (Proverbs 3:11–12).

I remember being shocked the first time I spanked my son. I don't remember what he did, but I gave him an appropriate spanking. Immediately after his spanking he flung his arms around my neck and said, "I'm sorry daddy. I love you!" I was shocked. I disciplined my son and he was telling me he loved me.

Our Father helped me to see that appropriate discipline done in love begets love. I love it!

Our Father is the Master Parent. He knows how to discipline us so that we learn what we need to learn and our love for Him is enflamed.

Beautiful.

Third, he will lead you to make whatever changes are necessary for you to make so that you can continue in faithful living. You may need to change the way you keep your finances. You may need to change how you spend your time. You may need to change your attitude about your role in your business or your marriage or another area of life. You may need to change the depth of your trust in God's faithfulness. Whatever changes need to be made, our Father will graciously lead you to do so.

When God drove Adam and Eve out from the garden, they did not argue with Him. They agreed with His changes and followed His lead. You will not make the changes in your own strength. The Holy Spirit will work with you to bring about the changes. Grace-living is not on you, it is on the Lord. As you rest in Him, He will lead. You follow His lead.

Encountering True Grace Inevitably and Eternally Changes You

To encounter grace is to be changed. You cannot come into contact with grace from the Creator and not be changed. Encountering grace is a hard-to-explain, supernatural experience that awakens a desire for more. Grace will make you humble and create in you a disposition of humility.

Who are you that the God of Creation, the One who hung the stars and the moons and the planets and the galaxies, would know your name, care about you, and love you? Who are you that He would give up His Son to be beaten by mere men, His creations no less, to pay for our selfishness? Who are you that He would love you as deeply as He does? Coming in to contact with grace exposes your weaknesses, your smallness, your vulnerability, and your need. You no longer hide, or run from, your imperfection. You now accept it and are blessed that Your Father loves you in your imperfection and mess. That humility frees you from all pretense of superiority or expertise in anything.

Humbled, grace then produces compassion in you. Because of the many years God has spent bringing you to your knees and the myriad ways He has broken you and breaks you, you are given great compassion for the plight of all people. You just understand pain and failure and shame and guilt because you have embraced yours.

Armed with compassion, the tone of your voice changes. You no longer pounce upon other's mistakes with vigor. Your words and your temperament reveal a veteran's experience of offering up your own mistakes to the Lord. The rebuke you give, and you will have to give, is no longer venom-filled.

Encountering grace also works to give you a glorious perspective. So many of us need to relax. There certainly are severe sins that require a serious response. But the majority of what we deal with in our lives and in our marriages do not warrant what we do. Consider that Adam and Eve's sin handed over all of creation to Satan, severed the pristine relationship between them and the Father, Son, and Holy Spirit, and corrupted men and women for life until Jesus returns. What exactly did your spouse do that was so bad?

Living in leather, walking in grace, and allowing our Father to deal with your issues is life-giving. You need to allow our Father to teach you as an individual how to receive grace from Him for yourself. God wants to create a culture of grace in your relationship with Him so that He can address specific issues in grace.

As you allow Him to treat you with grace, then you will begin to treat yourself with grace. I think the way of grace is so foreign to us that it takes the power of the Holy Spirit to undo everything we have learned and re-wire us. Learning to walk in grace happens one God-forgiven mistake at a time. In the beginning we are still hiding behind the bushes. Slowly, we are brought out and now live our lives in the freedom of grace, not in the folly of some kind of I-can-sin-because-of-grace, but in the maturity of Christ-given liberty that trusts how our Father deals with our sin.

Filled with grace, you can learn to treat your spouse with grace. You want to ask the Lord to create a culture of grace in your marriage so that, no matter what the issues are, they can be addressed in grace. **Do not wait for your spouse to go first, and do not wait for them to deserve your grace.** God did not wait for you to go first, and He certainly did not wait for you to deserve it.

Conclusion

The tyranny of performance is intense. Everywhere people strain to please parents, bosses, spouses, coworkers, and themselves. We are exhausted and overwhelmed. Marriage is barren because life has worn thin.

God our Father blows the gentle wind of grace through the harsh, under-performing condition of our hearts. He lifts us out of the thicket of our own efforts and blesses us with a new way to live. The way of grace is a way we must learn, for all our lives we have drunk from the fountain of our works. Grace can be unsettling and awkward at first. But God is a patient teacher.

Marriage is the joining together of two very imperfect persons. Imperfect people make mistakes! And they will continually make mistakes until they die! If you want your marriage to succeed, then learn how to receive God's grace for *your* mistakes. Then you will clearly see how to treat your spouse's ongoing mistakes the same way!

Even as you finish this chapter, I pray that you are already experiencing the loosening of grace in your soul. The Holy Spirit is inviting you to come out from behind the bush, lay your sins at your Father's feet, receive the forgiveness of Jesus, and be restored to intimacy and stability!

CHAPTER 5
FIGHT: ENGAGE IN SPIRITUAL WARFARE

Of all the marriage books, sermons, and conferences I have read, heard, been to, and heard about, there is one glaring omission in the material covered. The omission is frustrating to me because I believe many lives and marriages are torn apart because of it. What has been left out describes the condition of the world we live in. It lays out the real context of humanity that, when rightly understood, explains so much.

The great omission is spiritual warfare.

I don't know how you're responding to that statement, but consider these things:

- Adam and Eve's first marital problem was caused by Satan.

- Jesus dealt with demons all throughout His ministry, even going one-on-one with Satan himself.

- Right after Paul's words on marriage in Ephesians 5, which may be the most popular biblical verses on marriage, Paul exhorts followers of Jesus, in Ephesians 6:10, "Put on the full armor of God, so that you will be able to stand firm against the schemes of the devil." Notice Paul trains his disciples to put on armor. He does not say that we are to put on a dress or football pads or a business suit. Spiritual warfare is so violent that we need armor. This is not child's play and everything is at stake.

How much more evidence do you need of the legitimacy of Satan and his present, destructive work in life and marriage? Have you ever considered that the source of your marital issues may be a demonic attack? Have you ever considered that the reason why none of the counseling you have gone to, the pharmaceuticals you have taken, or the books you have read have worked is because the root of your issue is supernatural? Remember, we have been made a holistic duality, a divine mix of body and spirit.

This is not to say that Satan, or one of his demons, personally stirs up each one of your issues. As we saw in Chapter 4, we are very capable of egregiously sinning all on our own. But we are foolish as followers of Jesus if we blow off or minimize Satan's presence in this world. The Apostle John writes in 1 John 5:19, "We know that we are of God, and that the whole world lies in the power of the evil one."

Engage in spiritual warfare.
The keyword for this lesson is **fight**.

If we are going to walk with God, then we are going to have to learn how to fight. Regardless of how we feel about living at war (I don't like it at all), Scripture is clear that we do. We must be trained how to fight. The psalmist writes, "Blessed be the Lord, my rock, who trains my hands for war, and my fingers for battle" (Psalm 144:1).

So let's get to training.

Where the War Began

Adam and Eve have been richly and completely blessed by God Himself. They are alive, in perfect relationship with the Father, Son, and Holy Spirit, and living in the immaculate garden of Eden. As we have seen in previous chapters, God gave them His divine command, "Be fruitful and multiply, and fill the earth, and subdue it" (Genesis 1:28). Our Father also warned them, "From any tree of the garden you may eat freely; but from the tree of the knowledge of good and evil you shall not eat, for in the day you eat from it you will surely die" (Genesis 2:16–17).

So Adam and Eve lived in the presence of God, able to see Him and relate with Him in a purity that has not been experienced since. They have revelation from God for direction and morality. They have God's word. Everything is set for a great life.

And then . . .

"Now the serpent was more crafty than any beast of the field which the Lord God had made. And he said to the woman, 'Indeed, has God said, "You shall not eat from any tree of the garden"?'" (Genesis 3:1). A creature appeared in the garden and began talking with Eve, questioning her about what God really said to them.

Instead of rejecting the serpent, Eve carries on a short dialogue with him. With just one question and one statement, this more-crafty-than-any-beast-of-the-field serpent undoes the magnificence of all that God has made. He convinced Adam and Eve to eat from the one tree God commanded them not to eat. The innocence of the relationship between God and man was soiled. The serenity of the garden of Eden and the perfection of what God had built was corrupted. Adam and Eve, once intimately beholden to God and each other, are now hiding in bushes and pointing fingers at each other.

How did this happen?
Adam and Eve knew the presence of God and the word of God.
Can you see what they didn't do?

They didn't fight. They didn't stand for God's word and His way in life. They didn't reject lies. They didn't rebuke this strange enemy who showed up in the garden one day and started questioning the wisdom and plan of their Father. They gave into temptation and justified their way to compromising their faith.

One question.
One statement.
It was *that* easy.

If we are going to succeed in our lives and in our marriages, we need to gain wisdom in how this enemy works so that we can stand, fight, and win.

The Mastermind Behind the War

Moses uses one word to describe the serpent. In the Hebrew, the word is pronounced aw-room. In English the word means, "shrewd, crafty." Shrewd is defined as "astute or sharp in practical matters."[6] Someone who is crafty is "skillful in underhand or evil schemes."[7] The picture of Satan depicts a person who carefully plans out an attack based on perceived vulnerabilities.

In the New Testament, Peter describes Satan as a "roaring lion" prowling around "seeking someone to devour" (1 Peter 5:8). Lions typically hunt at night or in the early morning. One of their strategies is to lie in wait around a water source. Lions can be very patient predators looking for the right time and place where their prey will be most vulnerable. Lions attack for no other reason than to kill their prey.

Paul describes Satan as one who "disguises himself as an angel of light" (2 Corinthians 11:14). To disguise oneself is to "change the appearance or guise of so as to conceal identity or mislead."[8] Satan will take any form required to most effectively lead people away from God's holy truth and love. Satan is a master combatant and deceiver.

---

[6] "shrewd," http://www.dictionary.com/browse/shrewd
[7] "crafty," http://www.dictionary.com/browse/crafty
[8] "disguise," http://www.dictionary.com/browse/disguise

Consider the guile of Satan in light of his ability to convince other angels to follow him. When Lucifer fell, God kicked him out of the regular, freely accessed presence in the Divine Assembly. Evicted from the purity of the love of the Father, Son, and Holy Spirit, Lucifer (now Satan) convinced one-third of the angels that they should leave God's side and join him.

That is how powerfully deceptive Satan is. He convinced a third of the angels, who could see the manifest presence of the Triune God, that following him would be better.

If the attacks of Satan were limited to some celestial sphere where we, as followers of Jesus, were unaffected, then this chapter would be useless. However, that is not the case. From the beginning, this Ancient Deceiver of man set his lion eyes on God's people. He came to destroy the intimacy that Adam and Eve had with God *and* each other.

You need to come to terms with the reality that Satan does not care about you. He does not care how much pain you are in. If your mom died today, he will be right there compounding your rage because of something else one of your family members is doing.

He is relentless, harsh, brutal, and determined. He will use any manipulation and vulnerability he can exploit and he will not stop until he succeeds.

If we learn anything about the war from the garden of Eden, it is that we need to respect Satan's deceptive ability and lose all our arrogance that somehow he is not able to fool us.

His First Battle, Our First Loss

Satan began his conversation with Eve by asking a question: "Indeed, has God said, 'You shall not eat from any tree of the garden'?" (Genesis 3:1). (Moses does not address the very odd reality of an animal talking. Maybe Eve was unsurprised because she was still discovering many of the wonders of the garden and counted talking animals as one feature she hadn't yet discovered.) There can be too much read into Satan's strategy of pursuing Eve first instead of Adam. That Satan approached Eve does not mean that women are weak and are always the way Satan gets in. Satan is too crafty to adopt the same strategy every time. Approaching Eve was just the first strategy Satan used.

So he has Eve thinking through what God said. He is probing how much clarity Eve has about God's word for her life.

Eve replies, "From the fruit of the trees of the garden we may eat; but from the fruit of the tree which is in the middle of the garden, God has said, 'You shall not eat from it or touch it, or you will die'" (Genesis 3:2–3). It is certainly true that Eve has added "Do not touch" to God's command, "Do not eat." That may be evidence of Eve feeling the burden of God's limitations. However, that is not what Satan targets. Remember, Satan is a master hunter who is looking for vulnerabilities to seize. If Eve's addition is important, Satan chose not to attack it, instead going after something else.

He says, "You surely will not die! For God knows that in the day you eat from it your eyes will be opened and you will be like God, knowing good and evil." (Genesis 3:4–5). Satan probes Eve's belief in whether or not she will actually die. "You don't believe you are actually going to die?" You can hear the sarcasm in his voice, "There is no way you can believe that!"

While she is considering the truthfulness of her potential death, Satan shifts gears and offers an alternative outcome. He tempts Eve with a new, enlightened condition that she is not experiencing now. "Your eyes will be opened and you will be like God, knowing good and evil" (Genesis 3:5). In other words, "You can be *more* than what you are. There is so much *more* to life. You can have it *here and now*."

We can call this technique of Satan his "here-and-now" approach. Satan tempted Eve with an opportunity to immediately experience something more. She did not have to wait on God. In Satan's option, Eve could do what she wanted when she wanted and the promised result was to be fantastic.

Maybe you will recognize this line of thinking: "You can have sex now. What God really cares about is two people loving each other. There is so much more for you to experience. Look at how handsome/beautiful they are. Nothing bad is going to happen if you do this. And you can have this more *here and now*." Or maybe you will recognize one of these: "You can have more house, more reputation, more status, more money, more beauty, and on."

The here-and-now temptation to more is powerful.

Notice Satan's temptation was not to deny God. You could have asked Eve at any point in her downward way if she believed in God and she would have said yes. Satan's temptation was slicker than that. She believed but she was not content. He stirred in her an opportunity to have more.

How Eve ends up in her sin is interesting to observe. She does not jump straight to disobedience. She convinces herself that eating the fruit is justified. "When the woman saw that the tree was good for food, and that it was a delight to the eyes, and that the tree was desirable to make one wise, she took from its fruit and ate" (Genesis 3:6).

She saw that the tree was good for food—that is a blatant justification. "Good for food" has *nothing* to do with Satan's temptation. Satan did not tempt her with her need to eat food; he tempted her with her desire for instant wisdom. Seeing that the tree was good for food means Eve was thinking, "Well, it does look good for food and God knows we need to eat." It also means her appetite kicked in. Her mouth started to water and her stomach began to argue with her head. Satan engaged her physical desires.

The tree was also a "delight to the eyes." Notice how the enemy entices Eve through her eyes. He gets her to look at the beautiful tree with its beautiful food. He is a master manipulator who will access all five of our senses to lure us away. Eve received pleasure when she looked at the delightful tree.

Finally, the tree was "desirable to make one wise." The tree was good, a delight, *and* desirable. Satan does not trot out some barren, devil-labeled fig tree. He knows what he is doing. He offers Eve wisdom. He tempts her with an ability to experience life on her own, apart from God.

She falls and eats.
The prowling lion gets his prey.
The masquerading angel deceives a soul.

And then, to compound the tragedy, "She gave also to her husband with her, and he ate" (Genesis 3:6b). With no explanation of his decision, Moses simply says that Eve gave the food to Adam and he ate. He put up no fight. There was no struggle. He just did what his wife had done. Satan took out two birds with one piece of fruit.

Man and woman were separated from God and from each other. Guilt, fear, insecurity, and instability were the new normal. And now Adam and Eve are finger-pointing, denying, and blaming.

The first marriage was torn because of a spiritual attack that neither Adam nor Eve fought against. Both Adam and Eve had personal responsibility to stand firm against the attack. Eve should have said, "No!" She did not and brought her sin into marriage. Adam should have said, "No!" He did not and his sin brought pain and suffering. (If it is true as the passage suggests that Adam was standing there when Eve had this conversation with the serpent, then Adam is even more responsible. To think that he never spoke against the serpent as he stood there and watched his wife get deceived is tough.)

Had Adam and Eve handled the demonic temptation correctly, their marriage would not have suffered. They did not fight.

A War of Words: Jesus vs. Satan

Thankfully, Jesus shows us a different way. In between His baptism and the start of His public ministry, Jesus was led by the Spirit into the wilderness for forty days. Satan came and tempted Jesus in that wilderness. Just as Satan sought to lead Adam and Eve from the love and faithfulness of God, so too he sought to do the same to Jesus. I offer here a summary of that interaction. A detailed description can be found in the first appendix.

Satan tried three different ways to tempt Jesus. Each temptation helps us to see another way in which Satan will try and tempt us away.

In his first temptation, found in Luke 4:2–4, Satan tempts Jesus with what we call "The Satisfied Life." Jesus was hungry. Satan tempted Jesus to use His power, apart from the will of His Father, to turn a stone into bread and satisfy Himself. Jesus shot down this attack saying, "Man does not live on bread alone but on every word that comes from the mouth of God" (Deuteronomy 8:3). Where Adam and Eve failed to stand on God's Word, Jesus succeeded.

Satan, however, did not go away. He simply sought another weakness. In his second temptation, Satan tried Jesus with "The Great Life." Satan offered Jesus leadership over all the kingdoms of the world. He could have instant greatness. He could accomplish great things. And all the world would worship Him. All He had to do was worship Satan. Jesus declined, refuting the attack by quoting Deuteronomy 6:13, "You shall worship the Lord your God and serve Him only." Again, Jesus defeated the attack by standing on God's Word.

Satan tried a final possibility. In his third temptation, Satan tried Jesus with "The Special Life." Satan suggested Jesus was special and could do whatever He wanted, knowing that His Father would bail Him out. He could live free believing His Father would be faithful regardless. Jesus deflected this attempt to drive a wedge between Him and God by declaring, "You shall not put God to the test" (Deuteronomy 6:16).

In each of these encounters, Satan was suggesting ways of life to Jesus. Just like with Adam and Eve, Satan sought to separate Jesus from the love and faithfulness of His Father. He is a Master Deceiver who hates God, the plan of God, and the people of God.

Spiritual Warfare Will Infiltrate Your Marriage

Can you see how the enemy probes, looking for weaknesses, so that he can tempt to sin, separating you from our Father? The examples of Satan's work go in every direction possible. Satan can pervert every word of God and attempt to lead followers of Jesus into doubt, and ultimately away from the Lord.

I offer these as a few examples to show how his attacks can bring down your marriage:

- A husband is not content with his status in life. He is able to do more, have more, and become more. In order to fulfill his belief, he must work more. He begins to take on more assignments which take him away from his family. Any time his wife mentions wanting more time, the husband snaps and yells at his wife. He still believes in God but has believed the lie that he can have more, now.

- A wife falls prey to the demonic attack of "The Satisfied Life." She seeks satisfaction in her house, believing the lie that a wonderful house will bring her joy. The house has become her bread. Her life has become her house. She believes God is good in all things but believes she must have a wonderful house to be satisfied. She constantly pressures her husband and her children to keep the house spotless. She berates her family because of their laziness. She constantly looks for a new house and compares her house with those of her friends. She has no rest.

- A woman wants to constantly help people. Her life is dedicated to helping others in need. Her continual service leads her more and more away from her husband and family. She has believed the lie of the "Great Life." Godly deeds are replaced by great deeds. Many people start to look to her for direction. She has no rest because none of this is God's will for her life. Her husband is left on his own. Her kids feel the distance and the competition as mom's heart is regularly divided. She does not trust that God's will for her life will get her the recognition she now has or will give her the ability to help like she is helping.

- A husband continually worries about his family's financial situation. He scrutinizes every penny spent. He has no peace at all. Consequently, he yells at his wife and demeans his children. They do not understand what he is going through and the stress it causes. Unfortunately, the man does not realize he has believed the lie of the "Special Life," which puts him in a position where he can complain about God's faithfulness. Instead of resting in His Father's faithfulness, this man lives in the terror of the enemy's lie.

These are normal situations married couples deal with. There are many, many more. Each one of these was instigated in the spirit by a demon. Instead of standing firm on the truth of God's Word, these men and women gave into the lies. Tortured by the lies, these husbands and wives began taking out their choices on their marriages and families.

The prowling lion roared.
The masquerading angel deceived.

Wield the Word as Your Sword

In the beginning of this chapter I referred to the Apostle Paul's training on spiritual warfare in Ephesians 6. After his introductory statement about spiritual armor and the schemes of Satan, Paul goes on to detail what spiritual armor looks like. He concludes his description in 6:17: "And take the helmet of salvation, and *the sword of the Spirit which is the word of God*" (emphasis added). The Word of God is *the* sword of *the* Spirit. The Holy Spirit has a sword that He wields in warfare. His sword is *the* Word of God. His sword is truth. The Holy Spirit works to defeat the lies and deceptions of the enemy by responding with the truth of God's Word. The power of God is in the rightful use of the Word of God. As Jesus showed us, the enemy cannot stand against the Word of God. He must flee.

In fact, James trains his disciples the same way. He says in James 4:7, "Submit therefore to God. Resist the devil and he will flee from you." Satan must flee in the presence of a life that is submitted to God and His truth.

All Adam and Eve had to do was say, "No! God's word clearly said we were not to eat from the Tree of Knowledge of Good and Evil." Satan would have had to leave. Their relationship with God would have stayed intact. Their relationship with each other would have stayed intact.

The Word of God is our powerful sword of the Spirit. Learn it. Memorize it. Know the areas of your life where you are vulnerable and learn what God's Word has to say. As you are tempted by Satan or one of his cohort, do not give in to the lie. Stand in the Holy Spirit and declare God's Word to be true. This is how we fight. We fight by standing firm in the truth of God's Word, rejecting lies and accusations from the enemy. You are going to get hit. You are going to hear new lies, new accusations, and new deceptions. As the Spirit nourishes you on the Word of God, you will be equipped to refute each lie. You will experience the power of God's Word *for you* and your spouse will be a beneficiary of your Christ-given victory.

Quit following the deceptions of Satan.
And quit taking out his lies on your spouse.

Luke 4:13 is one of the most ominous verses of Scripture. After his three failed temptations, the Scripture says, "When the devil had finished every temptation, he left Him until an opportune time." Satan was going to keep trying to get Jesus. His goal was clear: separate Jesus from the love and faithfulness of His Father.

Satan is still working today. He has set his sights on you and your marriage. The only thing the enemy can do is suggest; he cannot do, and he cannot force anyone to do. To be sure, his suggestions are powerful and alluring. I am reminded that Eve fell with one question and one statement. We need to accept, with great humility, how quick we are to walk away from the love and faithfulness of the Father, Son, and Holy Spirit. One line in the hymn "Blessed Assurance" goes, "Prone to wander, Lord, I feel it, prone to leave the God I love."

Conclusion

We have all seen action movies where the hero gets into a situation where the enemy has him trapped in a seemingly inescapable position only to have the hero defeat an army of men. The hero never flinches. He does not fear the fight because he knows how to fight.

The same is true for us in the Kingdom. We do not fear the fight because we know how to fight. We do not fear because we are letting the Holy Spirit train us. We do not fear the war because we walk in the power and authority of Jesus. The hits we take make us wiser, leading us to a deeper understanding of our own vulnerabilities and to memorizing Scripture we need. We feel His power in us. We believe. And we carry that belief into our marriages.

Be wise in the Kingdom.

The war rages.

Do not let the Great Omission tear you and your marriage down another day.

CHAPTER 6
MERGE: CHOOSE ONENESS

There comes a moment in a wedding where the pastor will declare, "By the authority vested in me by God, I pronounce you husband and wife. You may kiss your bride." This is quite an incredible instance. For in that moment, in the eyes of God, that bride and groom become one. Something mystical, mysterious, and magical just happened. God created something that has never existed in creation until then. The two became one. A new "being" was formed.

God says it this way in Genesis 2:24: "For this reason a man shall leave his father and his mother, and be joined to his wife; and they shall become one flesh."

Jesus says it this way in Matthew 19:6: "So they are no longer two, but one flesh. What therefore God has joined together, let no man separate."

In that divine moment of the "I do," the hands of the Almighty God forge two people into a new creation. Marriage is not just a man and a woman deciding to come together because they are both attracted to each other. In the bigger picture, marriage is a work of the Father, Son, and Holy Spirit joining that man and woman together in divine providence and love.

The three biggest life-changers are becoming a Christian, getting married, and having children. Everything changes when a person gives his or her life to Christ. Everything changes again when a person gets married. And everything changes a third time when children come.

One constant in each of these is change. If you are not willing to change, you will not make it as a follower of Christ, a spouse, or a parent. Change is inherent. From the moment the pastor declares the two are one, the man and woman become something they have never been before: husband and wife, joined together on a journey they have never been on before: marriage.

There is nothing in life that marriage does not touch. Everything in the man's life and everything in the woman's life is affected.

In the previous chapters we have focused on the 1+1 part of the marriage equation. In this chapter we are going to look at the =1 part. We move from the "Who am I?" question to "Who are we?"

Be one.
The keyword in this lesson is **merge**.

Marriage merges two lives into one. Merging two of anything can be messy, let alone merging lives. Whatever ages a man and woman are when they get married, they are merging together that many years of life, which is comprised of thousands of likes, dislikes, habits, rhythms, hopes, dreams, desires, and more. The opportunities for merger disappointment and frustration are everywhere.

The degree of merging God intends in marriage is called "one flesh." The marriage merger is not just changing addresses, adding a roommate, sharing a bank account, and occasionally having sex. One flesh is deep—deeper than you have ever been before.

In the same way God had an original design for your life, He also has an original design for marriage. Marriage on the rock of Jesus happens when we faithfully live according to God's perfect design. So what is one flesh and what does it look like? How do two people become one?

What Does One Flesh Mean?

One flesh can be defined as a term used to describe the deep degree of intimacy to be experienced in a new, God-created "us." One-flesh intimacy happens as God brings two people together to give themselves completely to each other. Nothing is withheld. The man and woman both forsake the right to say, "This is mine." Money may be in separate accounts for practical reasons, but there is no "my money/your money." A husband and wife certainly need alone time, but there is no "I have a right to do whatever I want whenever I want and you just have to deal with it." One flesh is deep, intimate *togetherness*.

ONENESS

One flesh says, "I am giving you all of me." One flesh is not neutral. It is not saying, "At least I am not doing _____." One flesh is not two people holding hands supporting each other's individual visions. One flesh is not the husband marrying so that the wife can help him accomplish his vision. One flesh is not the wife marrying so that the husband can help the wife accomplish her vision. One flesh is man and woman being joined together by God for mutual intimacy. One flesh is us. The "I" does not disappear but it gets subsumed by the "we." "I" is now in context of "we."

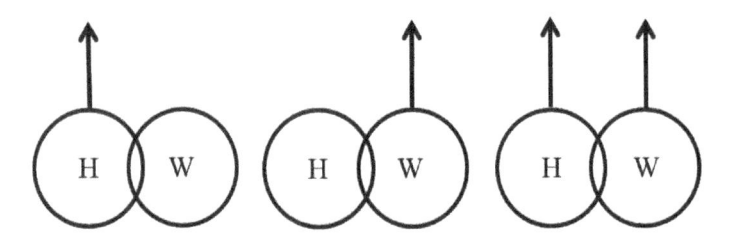

Figure 2: None of these represent one flesh.

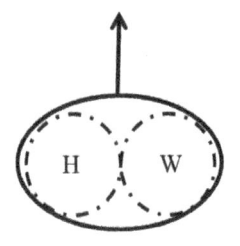

Figure 3: This represents God's one-flesh design.

On opposite ends of the marital spectrum are two phrases popular in the United States. One phrase says that a woman is supposed to be "barefoot and pregnant." Her role is confined to the house and the kitchen. Man runs the show. On the other end of the spectrum is the phrase, "If momma isn't happy, no one is happy." The climate of the family depends on how the wife is doing. Neither phrase is right, nor does either phrase describe God's one-flesh design.

Pursuing one flesh in your marriage is important because it is the will of the Father and the work of the Holy Spirit. A couple will ask, "What is God doing in our marriage?" While some of the specifics will be different at different times, one thing remains: God is at work to cultivate one-flesh intimacy in marriage. Whatever He is doing, He is developing intimacy. If you adopt some other understanding of marriage, you will cut off the will of the Father and grieve the work of the Holy Spirit. Conversely, if you embrace one flesh and lay that as your goal before the Father, then the full work of the Spirit will be available to you and your spouse to create and build a marriage lived on the rock of Jesus.

The power and the joy of one-flesh intimacy, and the freedom to vigorously pursue one-flesh intimacy, comes from the nature of God. The one God of all creation exists as three distinct persons: Father, Son, and Holy Spirit. Paul describes in 2 Corinthians 13:14, "The grace of the Lord Jesus Christ, and the love of God (the Father), and the fellowship of the Holy Spirit, be with you all." While they are distinct, they exist together in perfect, deep, pure love. Their relationship shows us the importance and power of deep intimacy. If we embrace the Trinity, then we should be liberated from all fear, awkwardness, and hesitation in giving ourselves to one-flesh intimacy. This is what God has made us for. Even for the one wounded deeply at the hands of maliciousness, the God of grace and healing works to lovingly draw us out of isolation and into safe, intimate love.

What's the Point of Marriage?

God's intent for intimacy in marriage is seen in the beginning with Adam and Eve. Why did God create Eve? He says in Genesis 2:18, "It is not good for the man to be alone; I will make him a helper suitable to him." God did not say, "It is not good for man to work by himself; I will make him a co-worker." He did not say, "Man is great, but I made him to be naturally sloppy. It is not good for man to be sloppy; I will make him a maid." (Brilliant!) And he did not say, "Man is the crowning jewel of the universe; I will make him someone he can dominate and intimidate. I will make him a dog."

God said man was alone. Man was not lonely. He was just alone. He had no one of his kind to relate to. Imagine all of creation from the expanse of the universe to the stars and the planets and earth. See all of earth in the beginning with the giraffes, monkeys, birds, alligators, fish, and the rest of the animals. In the midst of the amazing garden of Eden is Adam—all by himself. No one else is like him in all of God's creation.

Man had no one. God says, "I will make a helper suitable to him" (Genesis 2:18).

Marriage was made for intimacy!

Adam was no longer alone. Did God have work for them to do? Of course. But the priority of the marriage was intimacy. And, by the way, Eve was not just made for Adam; Adam was also made for Eve. As Adam was made for intimacy, so too was Eve.

The intimacy of one flesh is further seen in how God made Eve. While Adam was made from the dust of the ground, Eve was made from the rib of Adam. "So the Lord God caused a deep sleep to fall upon the man, and he slept; then He took one of his ribs and closed up the flesh at that place. The Lord fashioned into a man the rib which he had taken from the man" (Genesis 2:21–22). God did not make Eve from dirt like Adam. He made her from him. They are of the same "stuff."

In this way, Adam could say to Eve, "You came from me. I am of you. We are of each other." Adam and Eve were not just of the same kind, both human, they were *of* each other. The only way Adam could express this was to exclaim, "This is now bone of my bones, And flesh of my flesh" (Genesis 2:23).

More than just a recognition of physical similarities and correspondences, this was a declaration of complete vulnerability. "With everything in me that is me, I am yours and you are mine." Scripture says that Adam and Eve stood before each other "naked and . . . not ashamed" (Genesis 2:25). Nothing was hidden. Nothing was held back. In every way they were as individuals, they gave themselves to each other.

Adam's understanding of one flesh carried through to the name he gave God's new creation. Adam follows his flesh and bones exclamation by saying, "She shall be called Woman, Because she was taken from Man" (Genesis 2:23). The Hebrew for man in this verse is *ish*. The Hebrew for woman is *ish-sha*. That woman is a derivative of man is no slight on woman. Quite the contrary. The closeness of the names reflects Adam's understanding of the intimacy God intends them to have. Even in name they are to be intimately connected!

All of this talk of oneness between Adam and Eve is consummated through sex. "For this reason a man shall leave his father and his mother, and be joined to his wife; and they shall become one flesh" (Genesis 2:25). For what reason are the man and woman coming together? For intimacy! Because of intimacy a man will be joined to his wife. The verb "be joined" carries the imagery of soldering together two pieces of metal to form one new piece. Sex is the expression of holistic intimacy. When Adam was joined to his wife, they had sex.

Finally, the original marriage shows us that one flesh means husbands and wives share one purpose. "God blessed them; and God said to them, 'Be fruitful and multiply, and fill the earth, and subdue it'" (Genesis 1:28). God's call for Adam and Eve was for Adam *and* Eve. The Scripture says, "God said to *them*" (Genesis 1:28, emphasis added). Adam and Eve were to pursue God's plans for them together.

The marriage of Adam and Eve helps us to understand the intensity of one flesh. One flesh is a depth of intimacy God intends husbands and wives to experience in a new God-created "us." How does one flesh in the first marriage impact your marriage? How does God's design inform your beliefs about marriage, being a husband, or being a wife? Let's look at the implications one flesh has on specific areas in your marriage. As we walk through each implication, consider how the Holy Spirit may be re-shaping your beliefs and practices about marriage.

I am intentionally building a strong case and clarity for one-flesh intimacy because it is God's intent, it is the place of blessing, and it is the direction of the Holy Spirit. One flesh is the will of the Father and the work of the Holy Spirit. Jesus did not just die to forgive you of your sins;

He died to forgive you of your sins so that you could be reconnected in intimacy with the Father, Son, and Holy Spirit. Intimacy is the work of Jesus. Again I say, if you adopt any other understanding of marriage, then you cut off God Himself and His blessing cannot be upon you.

Embrace one flesh. Let the Holy Spirit heal you or correct you or deal with whatever in you needs to be dealt with so that your heart will be open to deeper intimacy than you have known.

So what does one-flesh intimacy look like? From the altar to the grave, how do a husband and a wife merge life? Let's look at some one flesh implications.

Marriage Requires Setting New Relational Priorities

The biggest change comes in the priorities of life. Once the wedding ceremony is over, the marriage becomes the highest priority in a person's life after their relationship with God and themselves. Every other relationship and pursuit falls in line behind the marriage.

After Adam sees Eve for the first time, the Scripture describes the change in Adam's priorities. Genesis 2:24 says, "For this reason a man shall leave his father and his mother, and be joined to his wife; and they shall become one flesh." Scripture says man and woman "leave" their parents and "join" to each other. Before marriage, the most important earthly relationship in a person's life is with their parents. Mom and Dad have more influence in life than anyone else. One flesh changes that. Momma's boy is no longer momma's boy. The boy needs to become the husband and the mom has to get out of the way. Daddy's girl is no longer daddy's girl. The girl needs to become a woman and dad needs to back out.

While it would be nice if mom and dad back out on their own, backing them out is the responsibility of the husband or the wife. If the husband's mom will not quit intruding, the husband needs to make her back out. One flesh says that a man has a greater responsibility as a husband than he does as a son. The same is true for the wife. From the altar forward, Mom and Dad fade into the relational background so that husband and wife can take center stage.

One flesh means there is no other relationship more important to each other.

This does not only apply to parents, but also to friends. Husbands and wives do not compete with anyone else for first place in their spouse's life. No one. The man is no longer "one of the guys" and the wife is not "one of the girls." That does not mean husbands and wives no longer have friends. But one flesh does mean that your marriage is more important. In one flesh, man and woman *both* say, "You are the most important person in the world to me. And there is not a second."
No one forced you to get married (or is forcing you to get married). Hopefully, when you got married you wanted to get married. And you wanted to marry whom you married.

What about past relationships? Please do not compare your marriage to past relationships. Please do not say, "Well, when _____ and I were dating, we did _____, and I think you and I should do that too." *No*! What kind of interaction can you have with those you have dated?

Tough question. Some of the answer depends on the comfort level of your spouse. No matter what kind of interaction you have, one flesh means you cannot reminisce in any way with those you have dated before. You do not share memories or recall good times. If you have memorabilia of any kind that reminds you of previous relationships, you need to throw it out. Those things may belong to you, but they have no place in "us." And they certainly have no place in "our" house.

At the altar, both man and woman say, "Life now becomes us and then everyone else." What conversations do you need to have to get your relational priorities correct? For the difficult conversations, ask the Holy Spirit to guide you in your words, tone, and timing. Remember, He wants to lead you and your spouse in one flesh. Reap the benefit of His leadership.

Marriage Requires Always Getting Better at Communication

If you want to succeed in marriage, learn how to communicate with your spouse. Communication is oxygen to intimacy; without it you will not make it. Learning to communicate well with your spouse so that you can talk about any topic equips you for the chaos, unpredictability, and difficulty of life. Life is hard and messy on your own. Now you are adding another life! Learn to communicate with each other.

Because no two people are the same there is no generic formula for communicating that you can plug yourself and your spouse into that will work for all occasions. Learning to communicate involves learning yourself and learning your spouse. Most spouses operate from some form of extra-sensory perception (ESP). We want our husband or wife to "get" us, know what we want, and get busy making it happen. ESP does not work.

Scripture gives us some great insight into how to communicate well. Again, this is not a formula, but it is the type of person the Holy Spirit is transforming us into.

In his letter to the church in Ephesus, Paul trains his disciples how those who are born again should communicate with each other. He writes,

> Therefore (since you have been made new), laying aside falsehood, speak truth each one of you with his neighbor, for we are members of one another. Be angry and do not sin; do not let the sun go down on your anger, and do not give the devil an opportunity (Ephesians 4:25–27).

Christ's transformative work in a person's life extends to the way they communicate. You cannot be in Christ and communicate the way you did before. Furthermore, Paul knows that in a church, and in a marriage, people need to talk. Intimacy requires communication. So Paul trains his disciples in godly communication.

He gives us four components of godly communication. The first component is transformation. Verses 25–27 follow verses 17–24. In these verses Paul describes the new life every person is given when they come to Christ.

In the new life we are being "renewed in the spirit of your mind" (Ephesians 4:23). We are to "put on the new self, which in the likeness of God has been created in righteousness and holiness of the truth" (Ephesians 4:24). In Christ, we have been made new. Our communication is a manifestation of the new life we have.

Consequently, godly communication is something we learn as we learn to walk in Christ. We are no longer allowed to say, "This is just how I communicate." And we are no longer allowed to say, "This is how my family communicated growing up." But you are new in Christ. You have been transformed and are learning a new way of life in which you put on a new self. Therefore, led by the Holy Spirit, you are capable of learning God's way of communicating with your specific spouse. Remember, your marriage is a co-work of God and you. He knew what He was doing when He put you together. So He is at work in your communication so that you can talk well with each other.

The second component is tone. This is not complicated. You can be right on an issue and wrong in tone and still be wrong. Tone is crucial to godly communication. In verse 25, Paul says that communication is important because we are "members of one another." The word "members" in the Greek refers to body parts. Paul says that members of the church are members of one body. As such we should communicate with each other in a way that we want to be communicated with.

Furthermore, Paul writes in Ephesians 4:15 that we are to speak, "the truth *in love*" (emphasis added). In communication, tone is the attitude that we bring to the conversation. How many times are you put off by a friend, a coworker, or a spouse simply by their attitude? "I cannot even hear what you are saying because your attitude is so bad!" Paul says the attitude of godly communication is love. In fact, if what you are going to say does not come from love, then you are not allowed to speak!

That means you cannot speak with an attitude of condemnation, revenge, jealousy, pride, greed, uncontrolled anger, self-righteousness, or spite. Godly communication between a husband and a wife have nothing to do with any of these. Love is the tone of God's language.

The third component is truth. We have already seen Paul's call to be people of truth in both verses 15 and 25. Followers of Jesus are those who have been called out of the darkness of lies, deceit, half-truths, and exaggeration to walk in the light of truth. In order to walk in truth, we are to "lay aside falsehood" (Ephesians 4:25).

I was meeting with a couple one time when the husband got up and left the room. The wife was furious. From her perspective, what the man did was rude and offensive. She did not give her husband the benefit of the doubt or ask him what had happened. She perceived that he was wrong and began to yell at him. What she did not know was that he had received a text from a client who'd had a medical emergency.

I want to say this as clearly as I can: your perception can be an ongoing source of falsehood! There is a great lie in American culture that says, "Perception is reality." I cannot stand that saying. I amend it this way, "While perception *may be* reality, it is *not* necessarily truth." Many lives and marriages have suffered unnecessarily because of a rush to judgment based on perception. As followers of Jesus, we are people of truth. We are not to be swayed by perception.

One other source of falsehood can be our feelings. "This is just the way I feel." You must know that you can be deceived in your feelings! Again, as followers of Jesus, we are called to filter our feelings through the truth. Truth absolutely feels. There are powerful, wonderful emotional experiences in truth. Truth is not void of feeling. But feeling must be grounded in truth.

The fourth component of godly communication is timing. You can have the right tone and speak truth but do so in the wrong time and fail! Paul trains his disciples to be aware of timing in communication. "Be angry, and yet do not sin; do not let the sun go down on your anger, and do not give the devil an opportunity" (Ephesians 4:26–27). On the positive side, Paul says it is okay to get angry. But then he governs our anger with three negatives: do not sin, do not let the sun go down on your anger, and do not give the devil an opportunity.

So how do we get angry and not sin? Biblical anger happens when we remain in control and accomplish the will of God. Every instance of God's anger in the Old and New Testament show that He is always in control and is always advancing His will. Anger is never out-of-control rage that only accomplishes the spouse's will. James echoes Paul in James 1:19–20: "Be quick to hear, slow to speak, and slow to get angry; for the anger of man does not accomplish the righteousness of God." Slow anger that accomplishes the righteousness of God is biblical.

Godly communication focuses on timing to buffer against the toxicity of anger turned to sin. We are not to let the sun go down on our anger. That does not mean that we have to hash out issues at eleven at night. In fact, being exhausted is a terrible place to be for effective communication! Go to bed. Sleep well. Wake up in the morning and set time aside to talk. Paul's emphasis is on the urgency of communication because he knows the toxicity and temptation of anger. When we unnecessarily delay talking or attempt to sweep issues under the rug we give the devil an opportunity. Poor communication is an open wound for the poison of Satan.

Nothing in marriage is more important to marital success than communication. I do not have space in this book to cover all the areas of change that will happen in your marriage. You are going to have to talk about your finances, how you spend your time, vacations, holidays, where you'll live, what kind of house you'll buy, what kind of furniture you'll have, who does what chores, sex, the future, careers, kids, parenting, health issues, and so, so much more. There are great books available on each of these areas and, certainly, Scripture provides God's direction in each. Success in all of this comes from great, godly communication between a husband and a wife so that no matter what the issue is, you can talk through it together.

Marriage Requires Changing Your View on "Your" Finances

The changes that happen financially are so powerful that I want to give a brief word of direction here. In God's marriage, there is no "my money/your money." All of the money God blesses a husband and wife with is "our" money. Furthermore, the money God gives is to be used in honor of the Lord. How does God want us to use the blessings He has given us? Understand that your blessing and satisfaction is all a part of God's financial planning for your family. Be free from the lie that God's way for your life is not satisfying, that you have to hold some finances back for yourself and your family. Give it all to Him and trust Him!

I've only met one couple who did not need a financial budget. They are far more the exception than the rule. You need to budget. You need to talk through how much money you want to spend on different categories, what your priorities are, and what you want to fund. Until I got married, vacations were not important to me. I soon learned they were important to my wife, Brooke. But we never budgeted for them. When we did take one, it was financially stressful and not relaxing for me. We started budgeting for them and the financial pressure was gone.

Finally, your marriage is a worthwhile financial investment. I worked with a couple who was paying two times their mortgage so they could get out of debt. However, their marriage was falling apart. I asked them how much money they had spent on their marriage in the past two years. They said none. I told them they were going to end up debt-free and divorced. Their marriage did not last long enough to get debt-free. Budget date nights and other times where you and your spouse can enjoy each other!

Marriage Requires Sex!

In addition to your finances, I also want to spend some set apart time on sex. You need to understand this. Paul talks a great deal about sex in 1 Corinthians 7. He urges husbands and wives to have active sex lives, warning that depriving one another gives Satan room to work. "Stop depriving one another, except by agreement for a time, so that you may devote yourselves to prayer, and come together again, so that Satan will not tempt you because of your lack of self-control" (1 Corinthians 7:5). Earlier we saw that Satan targets couples in their communication. There is only one other area of life that Paul gives specific warning against satanic attack: sex.

Think about this as a litmus test for a great marriage: How many marriages do you know that have great communication and great sex? There are certainly other factors we can consider, but just anecdotally, how many marriages do you know that have great communication and great sex? I suggest that your anemic answer is because Satan is fully at work in these two areas.

Why? Why would Satan train his efforts on these two areas? Because sex and communication have everything to do with intimacy. One flesh is about intimacy. The Trinity is about intimacy. Salvation is about intimacy. Satan has been separated from God. He *hates* intimacy. Therefore, whatever he can do to bring division, to keep you from communicating and keep you from enjoying sex, he is going to do.

And sex is all about intimacy. In fact, sex is the highest expression of intimacy reserved for the blessings of marriage. Adam and Eve consummated their "one flesh" through sex. Paul recognizes the uniqueness of sex saying, "Every other sin that a man commits is outside the body, but the immoral man sins against his own body" (1 Corinthians 6:18). Sex is the unique, ongoing expression of intimacy between a husband and a wife.

Look at how Paul connects the depths of one flesh with marriage: "The wife does not have authority over her own body, but the husband does; and likewise also the husband does not have authority over his own body, but the wife does" (1 Corinthians 7:4). This passage can certainly be twisted for all sorts of unfortunate perversions.

This does not mean that a spouse can demand sex or abuse their husband/wife sexually. That is revolting to the Lord, and anyone who does so will stand before Him and be held accountable. "It is a dreadful thing to fall into the hands of the living God" (Hebrews 10:31). Mutual ownership is a beautiful trusting of another with your body. We graciously give our bodies to our spouses in loving intimacy with each other.

As the Trinity exists in spiritual oneness, as salvation is a holistic reconnection of God to man, as marriage is more than the physical joining of a man and woman, sex is more than a physical act that brings great physical pleasure. Sex is much, much deeper. Generations and cultures have wasted, thrown away, and ignorantly tossed aside the riches of sex. We have settled for Spam when we could be eating prime rib!

What keeps you from having a godly, one-flesh sex life? As you work through the first five lessons from the garden, you can see how each one, if left unchecked, can contribute to an ungodly sex life.

- If you don't accept God's definitions of sex, then you are not going to feel fulfilled in sex and will seek fulfillment elsewhere.

- If you don't like how you look and cannot accept that you are made in the image of God, you are going to have a tough time with sex.

- You do not understand how sin affects you, so you wear yourself out in fear, anxiety, and insecurity, resulting in no physical or emotional energy left for sex.

- Grace is unfamiliar to you. Everything you do depends on how you perform. You do not want to engage in sex because you are so exhausted from performing, and/or you fear this is just another area you are not going to measure up in.

- Spiritual warfare is not something you engage in. Consequently, you do not communicate well. You hold on to issues and do not discuss them. Separation gets further and further apart. You have no desire to have sex, or the sex you have is very distant.

Great sex can be a helpful barometer for how strong your intimacy is in your marriage. It is certainly not the only way to measure marital health, but it can be helpful.

Whatever your sexual past has been, whatever your thoughts and emotions are about sex now, God created sex to be a beautiful expression of intimacy between a husband and a wife. Therefore, Jesus died to redeem you from the lies of the world and the sins of your past. There is nothing He cannot transform.

Do not let the enemy rob you of treasure God created for you to enjoy! As we must learn how to communicate well with our spouses, so too we must learn how to have great sex.

Conclusion

I hope you are able to see that God's standard and design for marriage is impossible for you to attain on your own. One flesh is so intense, so deep, requires so much, and demands so much that you cannot do it on your own.

That should be liberating!

Being a great husband is not the husband's responsibility. Being a great wife is not the wife's responsibility. There is no fear of failure. There is no performance pressure. When the husband and wife give themselves to the leading of the Holy Spirit, **He will make them** into the kinds of spouses that God the Father is calling them to be.

Paul writes in 2 Corinthians 3:17–18,

> Now the Lord is the Spirit, and where the Spirit of the Lord is, there is liberty. But we all, with unveiled face, beholding as in a mirror the glory of the Lord, are being transformed into the same image from glory to glory, just as from the Lord, the Spirit.

The work of transforming followers of Jesus belongs to the Holy Spirit. He, and He alone, has the ability to change every man and woman to become a son or daughter of God and the husband or wife God has called them to be. Our dependency on God for our transformation is also taught by Jesus in John 15:5. Jesus says, "I am the vine, you are the branches; He who abides in Me and I in Him, he bears much fruit, *for apart from Me you can do nothing*" (emphasis added). We know that the Holy Spirit is the person of the Trinity who carries out the work of Jesus today. Apart from Him we can do nothing. We cannot be the husbands or the wives God calls us to be. However, in the Holy Spirit we can do everything. In the Holy Spirit He will make us continually become greater and greater husbands and wives.

God has called us to a one-flesh standard that is impossible to attain without Him. But, in Him, in the Holy Spirit, He will produce God's intended degree of intimacy that both husband and wife will enjoy for life!

I have counseled struggling couples who have said, "At least we do not yell at each other."

I've replied, "Maybe you should yell at each other."

Then they raise confused eyes to me. "Huh?"

Yelling or not yelling is not the issue. The issue in marriage is intimacy. Yelling is not good. But, better to yell and get to intimacy than exist silent and separated.

Marriage is a spectacular existence of deep intimacy where God literally makes two people into a new creation. He calls it one flesh.

Accepting one flesh as God's design will help you by giving you a standard by which you can gauge the healthiness of your marriage. Now you will be able to see when you or your spouse are drifting from each other. Now you can see where God is leading you and potentially understand what He is doing in you.

One flesh is not easy—not at all. One flesh takes work. Many, many marriages will not make it simply because one or both of the spouses are not willing to surrender things in them to become one. One flesh *requires* the work of the Holy Spirit. Do not be discouraged. You are not supposed to be able to simply figure out marriage and walk hand-in-hand through life whistling love songs. Trust what our Father is doing in you and in your spouse. Give Him greater access to your life.

Ask Him to show you how to be a great husband or a great wife!

CHAPTER 7

JOURNEY: LEARN TO ROAD TRIP TOGETHER

I love a great road trip! There is just something about being in a car with good people, listening to music, enjoying life, and ambling down the road toward a cool destination. In college I took a road trip with a bunch of friends from Virginia Tech in Blacksburg, VA to Dallas for New Years, then to Telluride, Colorado, and we ended up in Las Vegas, Nevada. Simply put, it was an amazing trip.

Of course, a road trip raises many questions that have to be answered: Do I feel like going on a road trip? For how long? Whom do I want to go with? Do they want to go with me? Where do we want to go? How often are we going to stop? (You have to stop again?!) What kind of music are we going to listen to? Air conditioner or windows down? What are we going to do when we get there? Who's driving and what car are we taking? How are we paying for this?

On my college road trip, these questions were easy to answer because I took the trip with a bunch of guys. After a few grunts, we all agreed and were on the road!

However, in a marriage all of the questions now have to be answered by a man and a woman who can have completely different thoughts and dreams about the trip of their lives. And God designed marriage to be a "together-for-life" road trip. Two individual people journeying through life notice each other and begin to take an interest in each other. Over time they decide to spend the rest of their lives together. Knowingly or unknowingly, they join their journeys together. Two road trips become one.

Learn to road trip together.
The keyword for this lesson is **journey**.

In the last chapter we began to define the =1 in our marital algebra of 1+1=1. In this chapter we continue to answer the "who are we" question. Gaining understanding from the Garden about God's design for the journey He has for us will provide many answers to the "who are we" question. When we embrace those answers we can begin to enjoy the new rhythm of our joined road trip.

One Vision, Two Directives

Immediately after God created man and woman in His image, He commissioned them with two directives. Genesis 1:27–28 says, "God created man in His own image, in the image of God He created him; male and female He created them. God blessed them; and God said to them, 'Be fruitful and multiply, and fill the earth, and subdue it; and rule over the fish of the sea and over the birds of the sky and over every living thing that moves on the earth.'" First, God charges Adam and Eve to, "Be fruitful and multiply." Second, He commissions them to "fill the earth, and subdue it." The two directives are to build a family and to work.

So, God made Adam and Eve in His holy image to enjoy fellowship with Him as His son and daughter. They were to enjoy intimacy with the Father, Son, and Holy Spirit. They were placed in the abundance of the garden. They were given one to the other to experience a measure of divine oneness. Then they were given the mandates to join with God in the priority of family-building and co-laboring in work.

It is significant that God gave these directives to the man and the woman. While there are two directives, God has one vision for the first couple: marriage—a husband and wife pursuing God's vision for the newly created one-flesh entity. A man and woman journey *together* in the same *direction* toward the same *destination*. Furthermore, and this is critical, the vision for the couple is God's vision for the couple. God's mandates of family and work were not Adam's that he gave to Eve or Eve's that she gave to Adam. Family and work are the vision God gave to the couple. God did not create marriage for the man's ego or the woman's. God created marriage for a man and a woman to enjoy and journey together in His vision for them.

So marriage is not the man inviting the woman onto his road trip or the woman inviting the man onto hers. Marriage is not a husband and wife driving separate cars to different destinations but sharing the same garage. And marriage is not a man and woman in the same car constantly fighting over who gets to drive. Marriage is a man and a woman both yielded to the movement of our Father in them and walking out His vision together.

In Genesis 11:26, we are introduced to three brothers: Nahor, Haran, and Abram, who is married to Sarai. Their dad was Terah. They lived in a place called Ur in the land of some people called the Chaldeans. One day Terah decided to move the family west to a new land called Canaan. The family never made it. For some reason their journey was cut short and they ended up living in a land between Canaan and Ur.

Genesis 12 begins with God appearing to Terah's son Abram. Now, leading up to this we are given no indication that Terah or his son's actively worshipped or sought the face of God. So communicating with God was not an expectation or a regular practice in their family. Nevertheless, God shows up in Abram's life and tells him that He has a vision for his family. He commissions Abram, "Go forth from your country, and from your relatives and from your father's house, to the land which I will show you; and I will make you a great nation, and I will bless you, and make your name great; and so you shall be a blessing" (Genesis 12:1–2).

First, you have to imagine the scene of God appearing to Abram and what that would have looked like. But then you have to imagine what it would have looked like for Abram to tell Sarai that he heard a voice tell him that he and his family had to leave all of their extended family and move to a land they had never been to before.

Husbands, how would you approach that conversation?
Wives, how would you receive that?

What I want you to see is that God had one vision for the couple. The vision was not Abram's or Sarai's; it was God's vision. God's vision was not Abram's and it was not Sarai's; it was God's.

God has a vision for your marriage. His vision is not your vision and it is not your spouse's vision. It is His. Now that a man and woman's lives are merged together, the couple humbles themselves and seeks God's vision for their marriage. We have already learned from the garden that no matter the particulars of the destination, there will be two directives: work and family.

Father, Son, Holy Spirit, and Family

It is critical to include some space here on God's view of family. I say this as strongly as possible in the Lord: family is more important than work! I say this, in particular, for those in the United States and in other cultures where family has been made increasingly unimportant. In the United States, there is no question that work has become more important than family. Success is determined by a person's bank account and how high or fast they can climb the corporate ladder. The results of this perversion are devastating.

Consider this, please: God existed, before any act of work was done, in a Triune family. The classical definition of the Trinity is that God is one God who exists in three, distinct persons: the Father, Son, and Holy Spirit. Each was perfectly content in their love for each other. At some point, the Father chose to work to make creation.

Why? Why did the Father want to build? So that men and women could work a lot and love a little? No. So that these little, finite beings could labor and strive every day of their lives to see how big their names and reputations could get? Insane. The Father created so that men and women could enjoy life in His family.

This may be true in other cultures as well, but it is certainly true in the United States: we are addicted hyper-doers. We don't know how to stop, say no, be content, rest, slow down, or breathe. Everything must be done as much as you can as fast as you can to get as much as you can. Brutal.

God is Father, Son, and Holy Spirit. God is family. In the Lord, in the vision of God, in the direction of the Designer of Life, family is the crown jewel. Therefore, marriage is an eternally worthy investment of time, emotion, money, and energy. Therefore, family is an eternally worthy investment of time, emotion, money, and energy. If you want to see your life change and your marriage built on the rock, reject the lies of your world and embrace the godly significance of marriage and family.

Marriage is Lifelong

We need to look at one other aspect of this God-ordained journey before we consider God's roles and leadership. According to God's design, marriage is for one man and one woman *for life*. Divorce was never a part of the plan. The "for-life-oneness" provides the security both a husband and wife need to be vulnerable, learn, make mistakes, and grow together. Without the "for-life" commitment of oneness, the marriage experience comes with an underlying fear that the endeavor can fail on one side or an underlying belief that one can always leave if it gets too hard on the other.

God's "for-life" intent for marriage is seen in both Adam's "bone of my bones" (Genesis 2:23) declaration and in Genesis 2:24: "For this reason a man shall leave his father and his mother, and be joined to his wife; and they shall become one flesh."

Furthermore, the strength of God's desire is seen in Jesus' teaching in Matthew 19. Some Pharisees try to trap Jesus with a question about the legality of divorce. Jesus replies by quoting from the garden of Eden, "Have you not read that He who created them from the beginning made them male and female, and said, 'For this reason a man shall leave his father and his mother and be joined to his wife, and the two shall become one flesh?'" The Pharisees then ask why Moses allowed for divorce. "Because of your hardness of heart," Jesus said (Matthew 19:8). Then he adds, "And I say to you, whoever divorces his wife, except for immorality, and marries another woman commits adultery" (Matthew 19:9).

The disciples get the standard Jesus just reestablished for marriage. Their struggle with what Jesus just taught comes screaming through their response. "If the relationship of the man with his wife is like this, it is better not to marry" (Matthew 19:10). Get that: the disciples' response to Jesus's teaching is that maybe being single is not so bad!

Jesus does not relent. In verses 11–12, He basically says that marriage is not for everyone. Some people are eunuchs! *Eunuchs!* That is Jesus's response to the disciples' struggle with the garden of Eden standard of marriage. Jesus understands the "for-life" marriage design and does not lower the standard.

Embarking on this road-trip-for-life called marriage makes you vulnerable. You need to be able to share your heart, lean on each other, be free to be yourself without fear of condemnation or rejection, and live together fiercely. If either spouse constantly has a foot out the door, is always looking out for themselves, or is always holding back "just in case," then the marriage is doomed to fail from the beginning. Road-tripping together for life allows each person to fully embrace who God has made them to be and learn by grace (that means make mistakes) how to be a husband or a wife.

Different Roles

Having laid the groundwork of God's view on family and the "for-life" commitment of marriage, we can now turn to the roles God has for man and woman. Whether these roles are popular or not or whether they meet up with the latest statistics or trends or not is irrelevant. In the beginning, God knew what He was doing. And God's established will is that men and women experience fullness of life.

In John 15, Jesus uses a vine and a branch to help His disciples (and us) understand what following Him means. He says, "I am the vine, you are the branches; he who abides in Me and I in him, he bears much fruit, for apart from Me you can do nothing" (John 15:5). He follows that with, "These things I have spoken to you so that My joy may be in you and your joy may be made full" (John 15:11).

The vine/branch analogy is another picture of life on the rock we have discussed throughout this book. The way of life in Christ, the revelation of God from Genesis to Revelation, is life and joy and fullness. There will be learning and relearning for all of us who convert to Jesus and His way of life. Nevertheless, with each new lesson we will experience the joy of His presence and of our fulfilling our God-given design.

In His design, God has called the man to primarily focus his time on work and provision. The woman is called to primarily focus her time on building the family. Both man and woman are uniquely gifted with abilities to succeed in fulfilling these divine mandates. It is unfortunate how badly these have been perverted and misunderstood. So we will continue to look to Scripture as our guide and our dictionary, declaring, "As for God, his way is perfect: The Lord's word is flawless; He shields all who take refuge in him" (Psalm 18:30, NIV).

Our understanding of these roles comes straight from the garden of Eden. As we discovered in Chapter 3, God made men and women after a certain design. In that design, both men and women reflect the image of God, are made body and spirit, are children of God, and are blessed. However, differences exist between the genders. It is important to understand that differences do not mean differences in value. In the same way there are differences between the Father, Son, and Holy Spirit but all are equal, so too there are differences between men and women.

The Apostle Peter trains husbands to live with their wives "in an understanding way, as with someone weaker, since she is a woman; and show her honor as a fellow heir of the grace of life, so that your prayers will not be hindered" (1 Peter 3:7). Peter acknowledges that while there is a difference—men are physically stronger than women—that difference has nothing to do with value. Women are equal heirs of the grace of life. Peter strongly warns men that treating women unequally will neuter a man's prayer life! Believing Peter was led by the Holy Spirit to write these words, they take on the power of God Himself, rejecting any attempt by man to elevate his importance over his wife.

So differences can be embraced and enjoyed instead of feared and abused. Men and women are equal but different.

Men are built to handle the rigors of life outside the house in the provision of food and material to sustain life. Women are built to handle the rigors of life inside the house in the nurturing of life. The simple evidence is the biological differences God created between men and women. Men are built to be physically stronger. Women's bodies are built not only to birth children but also to nurture them (breast-feeding). If God wanted different outcomes, He could have made woman with the birthing parts and man with the nurturing parts or vice versa. He could have made reproduction happen in a completely different way. Nevertheless, God made man and woman exactly as He desired, with great, holistic, blessed intent. When followed, God's way of life produces intimacy with Him and fulfillment for the man and woman.

A second piece of evidence supporting these roles comes from the curses God imposes on man and woman in Genesis 3. We covered these in detail in Chapter 4. Here I add the detail that God cursed both man and woman in the place of His designed call. Women are cursed in the home and family; men are cursed in the marketplace. God did this in His infinite wisdom to require us to rest in Him for wholeness in the core roles He has made us for. A woman cannot feel secure as a wife or a mother apart from faithfulness to the Lord. Similarly, a man cannot feel secure in his work about from faithfulness to the Lord.

God lays out a clear plan for the differing roles of men and women in marriage in Genesis 1–3. Unfortunately, our families and cultures are filled with lies, perversions, and misconceptions that war against men and women living out these roles in spirit and truth. Let's confront some of those here:

- Anyone seeking fulfillment from any role other than being a child of God is going to be disappointed. Fulfillment does not come from the marketplace, a great paycheck, a beautiful house, or well-behaved children. One cannot find themselves in anything or anyone expect God alone. Fulfillment comes only from being made a child of God through the love of Jesus Christ and the presence of the Holy Spirit.

- For a woman, any sense of emptiness for devoting her life to faithfully building a godly home and family instead of being in the marketplace is not from the Lord.

- Women who choose to stay at home can have great economic fear because of their choice. If the marriage derails, then the woman has little marketability for entering the labor force. However, when the marriage is bound in the security of "for-life" oneness, the woman no longer has to fear and can relax into her divine role.

- These roles do not mean that men do not need to help in the house. Jokes about men not knowing how to change diapers are not funny; they are stupid. Men have valuable responsibility in the home and need to follow the leading of the Spirit in becoming the best husband the Spirit is making him to be.

- These roles do not mean that women cannot work. Certainly, when the couple does not have children the woman is free to work as she can. However, God's design does mean that when the couple has children, their care and nurturing is the woman's responsibility. As the children get older and their needs lessen, and a woman is able to care for the house with less effort, she is certainly available to pursue work. Proverbs 31 describes a woman who is able to care for her house and family and engage in the marketplace. Each couple needs to pray and discern the will of God and the capacity of the family situation in making decisions about when it is appropriate for a wife to go back to work.

God's design for marriage comes into sharper focus through the different roles. A husband and wife are to form a solid team with different roles. Working together, the husband and wife submit both of their wills and egos to the Lord to build a godly marriage and family. God's way works exceedingly well: both husband and wife are filled up in the Lord, the marriage is strong, the provisions are there, and the house is solid.

Leadership

Here is another topic that can cause all sorts of issues and fireworks. Both men and women can get very animated about God's leadership design for marriage. Men have abused this topic and many women have responded defiantly. We desperately need the Holy Spirit to breathe life and revelation into our marriages regarding leadership. Thousands of decisions, from large to minute, have to be made at the speed of life in marriage. Who is leading this thing? How do we make decisions? How is this supposed to work?

In the order of creation, man was made before woman. Genesis 2:15 says that God created man and put him in the garden. Woman was not yet made. Then God gave to Adam the commandment not to eat from the Tree of Knowledge of Good and Evil. God gave His vision for life to the man. After this, Eve was formed from Adam. While Adam is from dirt, Eve is from Adam. Then Satan came, tempted the woman, and everything fell apart. In the order of the Fall, Satan fell first, then Eve, and then Adam. God curses the three in the order in which they fell. Adam, saved till last, receives the greatest amount of rebuke.

God introduces Adam's curse: "Because you have listened to the voice of your wife, and have eaten from the tree about which I commanded you saying, 'You shall not eat from it . . .'" (Genesis 3:17). God reminds Adam that he received the commands and was responsible for leading his wife in obedience. God's rebuke does not mean that a husband is to never listen to his wife—that is an absurd conclusion. In fact, God's rebuke opens the door for the wife to check the man when he is not being faithful to God's word. God gave Adam his word. Adam was to stand strong in God's word and lead his wife accordingly.

The same pattern can be seen in the Old Testament. Noah, Abram, Isaac, Jacob, Joshua, David, and other men received direction from the Lord for their lives and their families. It is important to see that each of these men received God's vision for their families. As we have stated, the lives these men lived were not their own according to their dreams and desires. They had to let their dreams and desires die so that they could live out God's vision for them. And, equally important, their wives played pivotal roles in the *family obeying* God's leading. Sarai followed Abram to Canaan. Isaac's wife Rebekah played a remarkable role in ensuring the godly blessing of Abraham passed to the correct son, Jacob, and not Esau. (Her motives were certainly questionable, but the significance of her role is not.) Joshua's wife followed him into the Promised Land. Each husband and wife had to surrender themselves to God's leading for their marriages and their families.

Man as leader continues in the New Testament in the life of Jesus and the teachings of Peter and Paul. Jesus, born the Son of God, leads the church. There is no shame in the church following Jesus. In fact, the church experiences fullness through their submission to the Lord. Paul connects Jesus's leadership of the church with man's leadership in the marriage: "Wives, be subject to your own husbands, as to the Lord. For the husband is the head of the wife, as Christ also is the head of the church, He Himself being the Savior of the body" (Ephesians 5:23).

Please notice that Paul's definition of submission comes from the relationship between Jesus and the church. *The only acceptable picture of submission is the one that comes from how Jesus leads the church.* Men abusing their wives or church leaders abusing members is not what Paul is talking about. He is very, very clear that marital roles reflect the roles of Jesus and the church. Let us be wise in recognizing the work of the enemy to pervert the beauty of God's truth and His way of life.

Furthermore, Paul swiftly binds man's leadership to Jesus's love: "Husbands, love your wives, just as Christ also loved the church" (Ephesians 5:25). Just as the church is blessed and filled through the love and leading of Jesus, so too the woman is blessed and filled through the love and leading of the man. It is incumbent on all people in their obedience to any portion of God's revelation for life to allow God's Word to define what obedience looks like. Jesus's leadership of the church is marked by love—sacrificial, life-giving love. *Any form of male leadership in the marriage that does not fit this description is not of God and is to be rejected.* Jesus's love leadership creates space for the church to securely follow. A man's leadership of his wife should create the same space.

The testimony of Scripture from the garden of Eden to the life of Jesus and the teachings of the Apostles is uniform on the roles of marriage. Man is the primary receiver of direction for the marriage. As he humbles himself and asks God for revelation, he is wise to seek counsel from his wife. As the husband and wife walk in God's direction, the husband and wife encourage each other to be faithful to God's call. The woman can certainly receive insight along the way and the man is wise to consider her words.

The woman is fulfilled as the husband continually pursues her in love, setting the tone for the marriage. The man is fulfilled as the woman honors her husband in support of the vision God has for both of them.

No man or woman, and certainly no couple, can accomplish anything on their own compared to what God has for them. This is the glory of walking with God. In the Lord, your life and your work take on eternal significance, having been authored by God Himself. Having been rescued from the ways of the world, every man and woman, and then every marriage, has divine purpose and mission.

Let us recall that we believe, "In the beginning, God created…" (Genesis 1:1). We believe the Scripture is the revelation of the Almighty God. Some argue against biblical male leadership on the grounds that the teachings of these times reflect the culture in which these men and women lived. But this does not stand up if we believe that God is the Author of Scripture and the Designer of life. For God is not beholden to any culture or group of people. Rather, God is faithful to Himself in the wisdom of His design for His glory and the joy of His people.

The Great Leadership Issues

I've had many men complain about the pushiness of their wives, and I've seen many men be very absent from their leadership roles. To lead is to actively, intentionally lead. I've seen men try and lead by personality: "Quit worrying about everything. No matter what happens, I will take care of it." Eh? That's just not true, and that doesn't give a wife much assurance. Such a wife isn't allowed to ask questions and is just supposed to accept that such a man has considered everything and is fully equipped to handle whatever come—regardless of wherever it is that man's going that the wife isn't allowed to know. That kind of leadership does not work in marriage.

I've seen men who have no intentionality in their leadership. They never communicate where God is leading the marriage or the family. They never ask how the wife is doing on the road trip. They never bless their wives with assurance. When God called Abram and Sarai, Abram regularly needed assurance that God was still leading them and that He was going to be faithful. At one point, Sarai laughed at the thought that God was going to be faithful in their lives. If men are the primary receivers of God's Word and direction, then men need to be intentional in leading their wives. Men need to communicate God's direction. Men need to offer assurance as God assures them. Someone is going to lead. If a man does not intentionally lead his wife, she is going to fill in the void. And then he is going to complain about her!

Men, do you want to lead your wives well? Pursue Jesus with everything you have. Surrender. Ask God to speak to you. Demonstrate to your wife that you hear from the Lord and follow through in obedience to what He is leading *you* to do for yourself. Let her build trust in your ability to hear what the Lord is saying. Share with her how the Spirit moves in you through the Word. Tell her how the Lord used you in ministry in the office. Do not do these things so that she will see them or so that you will have something to tell her. Do them because your heart is zealous for the Lord and His kingdom. Lead your wife as Jesus led: intentionally and graciously in love. Lead in such a way that you create space for your wife to comfortably, securely follow.

I have also seen wives *refuse* to get out of the way so that their husbands can lead. "I'm not letting go of control of this." I've seen women nag and push and ridicule their husbands. I've seen women relentlessly pick apart their husbands and wives who do not give their husbands grace by continually reminding them of mistakes they have made.

All of our leadership issues must be left at the feet of Jesus. Life on the rock, marriage from the Garden, flows in a Spirit-led rhythm as men and women humble themselves under the mighty hand of God and become the husbands and wives God created them to be. Where you struggle in leading/following, ask the Lord to teach you. Ask the Lord for wisdom in specific areas of leading/following. Encourage your husband in his leadership. Assure your wife in her following. In doing so your marriage will be able to enjoy the faithfulness of God instead of experiencing the war of control.

Never Running Out

Brooke and I were visiting her family in New Jersey one summer. Her dad let us take his Corvette to the shore so that we could spend some time on the beach. We had a great time—I'd never driven a Corvette before! On the way back we ran out of gas. Oops! Here's the rub: the gas gauge said we still had a quarter-tank. When we finally got home, Brooke's dad told me that gauge doesn't work very well and you have to pay attention to the mileage. Lesson learned!

When a husband and a wife give themselves to God's road trip, they get to enjoy the freedom that comes from knowing God will never run out of what they need! He is *always, perfectly* faithful. The couple does not have to carry the burden of making it on their own. There is no pressure on the couple to provide or build a great family. On the road trip of God, God says that He is our provider and He is the builder of our lives. The gauges of God are never wrong and the tank of God is never empty!

After creating man and woman in His image and after His likeness, and after giving the couple His two directives, God tells them about the provision He has prepared for them. In Genesis 1:29–30,

> Behold, I have given you every plant yielding seed that is on the surface of all the earth, and every tree which has fruit yielding seed; it shall be food for you; and to every beast of the earth and toe very bird of the sky and to every thing that moves on the earth which has life, I have given every green plant for food.

God has not called husbands and wives to His road trip so that they would have to provide from themselves. One of the great benefits of living according to the will of God is that the couple gets to enjoy the faithful provision of God.

This has been God's plan from the beginning. It is no surprise that Jesus teaches the same thing. He teaches His disciples to pray the Lord's Prayer. In the Prayer we are taught to pray, "Your kingdom come. Your will be done, on earth as it is in heaven. Give us this day our daily bread" (Matthew 6:10–11). We are to pray for God's will to be done in our lives. As we are following His will, we are to pray for God to provide our daily bread. So we learn that the bread of God is in the will of God. When a husband and wife together seek the will of God, they are free from the fear of not having bread so that they can enjoy the faithfulness of God's provision. Many, many marriages suffer greatly and end because of the fear of not having bread.

Furthermore, marriages that follow the Lord's provision also enjoy the faithfulness of God in building their lives. The opening line of Psalm 127:1 captures the wonder of God's faithfulness to build lives: "Unless the Lord builds the house, they labor in vain who build it." God has plans. He has plans for life, for marriage, for family, and for each child in the family. In addition to being liberated from the fear of finances, the couple is liberated from fear and anxiety about the success of their children. On the road trip of the Lord, God is faithful to build the lives of those who trust in Him.

Peter declares in 1 Peter 5:6–7,

> Therefore, humble yourselves under the mighty hand of God, that He may exalt you at the proper time, casing all your anxiety on Him, because He cares for you.

Conclusion

Can you imagine a marriage lived in the faithfulness of God? In the beginning God knew what He was doing. And He still does! He created men and women to be co-equal with different roles. He created them to be one in marriage. And He created them to follow His leading so that they could enjoy His presence and His faithfulness. He is faithful to provide financially and faithful to produce great lives. What would marriage look like that uninhibitedly lived this way?

Do you remember what your car looks like after a road trip? You see all the bugs that have met their ends on your bumper and windshield. Your car looks more like you've been through a war zone than a trip to the beach. That's what marriage can feel like. Issues hit you faster than bugs on the road.

What you will find, or what you can re-discover, is that when the destination of your marriage is God's vision and not yours, and when men and women are fulfilling their God-created roles, then you have the right foundation upon which to deal with the curves, potholes, and bugs of life. The road trip of the Lord does not keep you from trial, suffering, or persecution. But the road trip of the Lord positions you in Him to experience fullness and strength that can endure any storm you and your marriage will encounter on the way.

A FINAL WORD

We learn from the garden of Eden that Adam and Eve were marked for God's purposes. Their lives belonged to Him for Him to do great work in and through them. Hebrews 11 is often called the Bible's Hall of Fame of Faith. Seventeen men *and women* are named in the chapter, all from the Old Testament. Every person listed is there because God had a powerful mission for their lives through which He would accomplish eternal work. They were faithful in spite of incredibly difficult challenges. The author writes in 11:36–38 about other, unnamed heroes of the faith:

> Others experienced mockings and scourgings, yes also chains and imprisonment. They were stoned, they were sawn in two, they were tempted, they were put to death with the sword; they went about in sheepskins, in goatskins, being destitute, afflicted, ill-treated (men of whom the world was not worthy), wandering in deserts and mountains and caves and holes in the ground.

In Hebrews 12, we are challenged to run the race Jesus has marked for us, to live by faith with the abandon those in Chapter 11 lived with, and to fix our eyes on Jesus so that we will not grow weary or lose heart, for we have "not yet resisted to the point of shedding blood in our striving against sin" (Hebrews12:4).

God has great, great work for you and your spouse. Walking with Jesus is not easy, not for the faint of heart, and not for the half-committed. But there is no other way to live. The way of life in Christ is glorious, powerful, truthful, and overwhelmingly satisfying.

From the garden of Eden we have sought to mine truths about how God has designed life and marriage. So many lives and marriages miss the fullness of what God has because they do not understand how He has designed life and marriage to work. I get that some of the teaching from the garden in this last chapter and throughout this book can be more than tough. Walking with the Lord is a journey. Marriage is a journey. "He who began a good work in you will perfect it until the day of Christ Jesus" (Philippians 1:6).

Seek Jesus in all things. Let Him be the rock of your life every day. Marriage geometry builds a triangle where both husband and wife pursue Jesus in their individual lives. As they each pursue Jesus, they grow closer and closer together. Marriage algebra teaches us that God's oneness equation is $1+1=1$, and He is the only one who can make that equation work. Let Jesus strengthen you, teach you, lead you, encourage you, and equip you to have a powerful life and, by extension, a powerful marriage. A man and woman become husband and wife to be loved by the Father, Son, and Holy Spirit and walk out their mission in life together. That is powerful!

A FINAL WORD

I pray that the Holy Spirit has helped you see some new things that have been negatively affecting your marriage.

I pray, if you are not yet married, that you are more equipped now to marry faithfully. Wait. Do not compromise in who you marry. Pray for one who has a demonstrated life of seeking the face and the will of God.

And, finally, I pray for you what Paul prayed for the brothers and sisters and husbands and wives at the church in Colossae in Colossians 1:9–12:

> For this reason also, since the day we heard of it, we have not ceased to pray for you and to ask that you may be filled with the knowledge of His will in all spiritual wisdom and understanding, so that you will walk in a manner worthy of the Lord, to please Him in all respects, bearing fruit in every good work and increasing in the knowledge of God; strengthened with all power, according to His glorious might, for the attaining of all steadfastness and patience; joyously giving thanks to the Father, who has qualified us to share in the inheritance of the saints in the Light.

ABOUT THE AUTHOR

JIM STERN is a pastor, speaker, consultant, and author. He leads CORE, a disciple-making movement in Houston, Texas, and founded Trexo, a discipleship consulting ministry.

He has written three other books:

- *Fortified: From Fear, Anxiety, and Bondage to Freedom and Power in Jesus*
- *Be: The Way of Rest*, the first of the three-part *Be, Go, Make* series
- *The On Ramp*

Jim lives in Houston, Texas, with his wife, Brooke, and his two kids, Collin and Claire. In addition to his love of authentically walking with Jesus and restoring people, Jim trains in Brazilian jiu-jitsu.

Visit his ministries at Corehouston.org and Trexo.org.